D0108669

WITHDRAWN

THE
CHICKEN
LITTLE
AGENDA

THE CHICKEN LITTLE AGENDA

DEBUNKING "EXPERTS'" LIES

ROBERT G. WILLISCROFT

PELICAN PUBLISHING COMPANY
Gretna 2006

Copyright © 2006
By Robert G. Williscroft
All rights reserved

The word "Pelican" and the depiction of a pelican are trademarks
of Pelican Publishing Company, Inc., and are registered in the
U.S. Patent and Trademark Office.

Library of Congress Cataloging-in-Publication Data

Williscroft, Robert G.
   The Chicken Little agenda : debunking "experts'" lies /
Robert G. Williscroft.
      p. cm.
   Includes index.
   ISBN-13: 978-1-58980-352-7 (alk. paper)
   1. Environmental ethics. 2. Environmental education. 3.
Environmental sciences—Political aspects. I. Title.
   GE42.W55 2006
   363.7—dc22

                                              2006007234

Printed in the United States of America
Published by Pelican Publishing Company, Inc.
1000 Burmaster Street, Gretna, Louisiana 70053

To Paul, who suggested this book;
to Michele, who nurtured it;
and to Mike, who missed its publication

Contents

CHAPTER 1

The Green Revolution

It is Tuesday, June 23, 1999. Capt. Joseph Hazelwood dons apron and gloves at the Bean's Cafe soup kitchen in Anchorage, Alaska. He works silently emptying lettuce into a container as part of his 1,000-hour community service sentence. Monday he loaded a truck with abandoned auto parts and assorted junk thrown along Anchorage roadways. He has a month to go, working off 200 hours of his sentence, one month a year for five years. By the end of his sentence he will be fifty-eight.

It began more than ten years earlier, at 9:12 in the evening on Thursday, March 23, 1989. Harbor Pilot William Murphy "had the conn" of the *Exxon Valdez* as she departed the Trans Alaska Pipeline terminal. With the help of a harbor tug, he guided her safely through the Valdez Narrows seven miles out. By 11:25 Murphy had yielded the conn to Captain Hazelwood and departed the ship. Hazelwood reported this fact to Vehicle Traffic Center and also reported the presence of many burgy bits—small icebergs from nearby Columbia Glacier—in the shipping channel. To avoid problems with the ice, he obtained permission to divert his track from the normal outbound channel across the separation zone into the inbound channel, and then he turned the bridge over to Third Mate Gregory Cousins. Before leaving the bridge, Captain Hazelwood instructed Cousins on exactly when to return the ship to its designated outbound shipping lane. The time was about five minutes to midnight.

Good Friday was just a few minutes old when Third Mate Cousins plotted a fix and determined that he should bring the *Exxon Valdez* back on track. About the same time, Lookout Maureen Jones reported that Bligh Reef light had appeared broad off the starboard bow. It should have been off the port bow; Cousins ordered a sharp right turn. Unfortunately, the *Exxon Valdez* was not yet up to normal cruising speed. She was sluggish in responding to Cousins' turn order. He was reporting the dire situation to Captain Hazelwood over the bridge telephone when the *Exxon Valdez* came to a jolting, grinding stop, hard aground atop a pinnacle at the edge of Bligh Reef. Eight of her eleven cargo tanks had been ripped open. The wind was blowing from the north at ten knots; it was just above freezing with a slight drizzle of rain and snow. Visibility was ten miles. Three hours and fifteen minutes later, 5.8 million gallons of crude oil had washed into Prince William Sound.

According to authorities, the final toll in southeast Alaska was 1,300 miles of beaches fouled by 10.8 million gallons of crude oil. Workers counted more than 35,000 dead birds and 1,000 dead sea otters after the spill, but since most carcasses sink, this is considered to be a small fraction of the actual death toll. The best estimates are: 250,000 seabirds, 2,800 sea otters, 300 harbor seals, 250 bald eagles, up to 22 killer whales, and billions of salmon and herring eggs.

A federal jury has slapped Captain Hazelwood and Exxon with civil penalties of close to a billion dollars for their alleged part in the Prince William Sound oil spill. Although Captain Hazelwood was charged with three counts of felony criminal mischief, and misdemeanor charges of operating a vessel while intoxicated, reckless endangerment, and negligent discharge of oil, he was convicted only of negligent discharge of oil, which normally would receive no sentence. In an apparent reaction to public outcry, Captain Hazelwood was awarded 1,000 hours of community service over a five-year period.

On October 9, 1991, the U.S. District Court approved the settlement among the State of Alaska, the United States government, and Exxon. The settlement resolved various criminal charges against Exxon as well as civil claims brought by both federal and state governments for recovery of natural resource damages.

Exxon received the largest fine ever imposed for an environmental crime: $150 million. Recognizing Exxon's heroic actions in cleaning up the spill and its voluntary payment of certain private claims, the court forgave $125 million of that fine. Exxon paid $12 million to the North American Wetlands Conservation Fund and $13 million to the national Victims of Crime Fund. Exxon also agreed to pay $100 million as restitution for the injuries caused to the fish, wildlife, and lands of the spill region. Finally, Exxon agreed to pay another $900 million over a ten-year period. This settlement contains a provision allowing the governments to claim as much as $100 million more to restore damaged resources, where that damage could not have been anticipated from data then available.

The Big Lie

Shortly after the spill in Prince William Sound, one news report described it as the worst manmade disaster since the bombing of Hiroshima. National headlines ranted against the huge, faceless, greedy corporation—the ogre that fouled the precious environment to save a few pennies on substandard ships and captains. The Sierra Club, Friends of the Earth, and other groups pounced on the apparent villains, focusing their anger on Exxon and Captain Hazelwood. They even organized "cut-ins," where everyone cut up their Exxon credit cards. They laid plans to bring about the indictment of corporate officers on criminal charges. It became the media event of the decade. More than ten years later, the Microsoft Encarta Online Encyclopedia joined the fray, reporting that "in March 1989 the *Exxon Valdez* oil tanker struck a reef in Prince William Sound and caused one of the largest oil spills in history." While these things make terrific news copy, and the headline boys love it, does this reflect reality?

Immediately after the Coast Guard arrived at the *Exxon Valdez* spill scene, the senior Coast Guard officer present requested that Captain Hazelwood remain aboard his ship to supervise ballasting to minimize the spill. He later testified that the captain was sober, alert, and fully capable of carrying out this task. In interviews conducted around the world following the spill, Captain Hazelwood was repeatedly described as the "finest tanker captain afloat," "one of the best, if not the best" ship's captain in the world, the "best captain I have ever served under," and "the best officer I have had serve under me." Admiration for this captain was unanimous and came from across the industry. From where, then, comes the nearly universal perception of this brilliant seagoing officer as an incompetent, lazy drunk?

The Alyeska Pipeline Service Company operates the oil terminal in Valdez. This company was formed by seven oil-producing firms. At the time of the spill, 50 percent was owned by British Petroleum through BP Pipelines, which controlled the company and was responsible for its operations. Sometime before the spill, Alyeska unaccountably removed thirty-six tons of cleanup equipment from the response barge located in Prince William Sound and stowed it ashore. Neither the Coast Guard nor the Port of Valdez raised a question when this happened. Subsequent investigation has revealed that all decisions concerning cleanup equipment and its maintenance and stowage were made in London by BP, *not* by Exxon.

Where was the Coast Guard when this equipment was moved ashore and put into storage?

Where were the Port of Valdez and the State of Alaska when London decided that keeping cleanup equipment at the ready was an unnecessary precaution?

What Really Happened

Exxon, of course, was on the scene. The men running this corporation sensed how the wind was blowing and made practical decisions. They spent more on the initial cleanup than the annual budget of several nations. Exxon deserves praise and respect for its actions following the spill. As it turned out, this was finally recognized by the court when it excused $125 million of Exxon's fine because of these actions. Nevertheless, the civil penalties levied against Hazelwood and Exxon are outrageous examples of how justice can be miscarried when emotion overcomes logic and opinion replaces fact.

Here are the facts.

Only 200 miles of Prince William coastline were significantly fouled, not 1,300 as "officially" reported, but this information appears only in the fine print at the end of the report. The remaining 1,100 miles received nothing more than possibly a light sheen of oil in one or two places along the beach.

While the general visibility was reported as ten nautical miles, the local visibility near Bligh Reef at the time of the grounding was near zero.

Far from being one of the largest oil spills in history, as reported in Microsoft's Encarta Online Encyclopedia, the Prince William Sound spill ranked a distant fifty-fourth. The *Amoco Cadiz* spilled nearly 70 million gallons of oil off the coast of Brittany, France, on March 16, 1978, over six times the oil spilled by the *Exxon Valdez,* and yet even this spill ranks only sixth. On June 3, 1979, the exploratory well IXTOC I blew in the Bay of Campeche off Ciudad del Carmen, Mexico, spewing 140 million gallons of oil into that beautiful bay. And even this ranks only number two. The all-time "winner" is former Iraqi leader Saddam Hussein, who caused the deliberate release of over 40.5 billion gallons of oil into the Persian Gulf, over 3,750 times the size of the Prince William Sound spill.

The Office of Response and Restoration of the National Oceanic and Atmospheric Administration (NOAA) reports on their Web site: "What we have found is that, despite the gloomy outlook in 1989, **the intertidal habitats of Prince William Sound have proved to be surprisingly resilient. Many shorelines that were heavily oiled and then intensively cleaned now appear much as they did before the spill.** Most gravel beaches where the sediments were excavated and pushed into the surf zone for cleansing have returned to their normal shape and sediment distribution patterns. Beaches that had been denuded of plants and animals by the toxic effects of oil and by the intense cleanup efforts show extensive recolonization and are similar in appearance to areas that were unoiled" (emphasis NOAA's).

In its evaluation of the effectiveness of the cleanup methods used after the spill, NOAA says: "Our intent in creating this monitoring program was to study shoreline ecological recovery after an environmental disaster like the *Exxon Valdez* spill, and then to use those lessons as scientific guidance for what we do in future response actions. At this point in time, our task is incomplete. However, **some of the findings have already changed the way we think about cleaning up oil spills"** (emphasis NOAA's). And then NOAA cites these examples (emphasis NOAA's):

- **More judiciousness in the use of aggressive cleanup methods,** such as hot-water washing, would help to temper the severe effects we have observed in biological communities.
- **Using water to flush an oil-contaminated beach may also wash away fine-grained sediments and nutrients** that small organisms need to successfully colonize; and it can take years for the fine sediment to return.
- Adult animals such as clams may survive in oil-contaminated beaches, but **juveniles do less well.**
- **Oil that penetrates deeply into beaches can remain relatively fresh for years and serve as a source of exposure to nearby animals.**
- After large-scale excavation or reworking of gravel beaches, **it can take many years for the beach sediments to recover.**
- **Rocky rubble shores should be of high priority for protection and cleanup** because of the potential for deep penetration and slow weathering.

What NOAA is really saying here is that the original problem was significantly exacerbated by the intensive cleanup efforts, however noble and well intentioned. It doesn't take brilliant insight to understand that oil covering the surface of rocks and sand is much less a problem than oil heated to low viscosity and forced down into the sediment by high-pressure, hot steam. This steam not only cleaned the rocks, it permanently destroyed the lichens and other vegetation that resided on them. As it turns out, most of these would have survived the oil had they simply been left alone.

The oil floating on the cold Prince William Sound

water tended to congeal into larger clumps of a tarlike substance. These clumps typically grew until they became sufficiently dense that they sank to the bottom, where they eventually were covered with silt. While this certainly poses some threat to the bottom critters near the clumps, for the most part the problem is relatively benign. By spraying the surface oil with detergents, however, the clumps never form. Envision television detergent ads wherein detergent-treated dishwater holds grease in suspension so that it does not stick to plates. In the ocean, detergent disperses oil in the same manner: the oil suspends in the water instead of floating on top, where it could be skimmed away. Consequently, it gets ingested by birds and fish. Even after as much oil as possible is soaked up into rags and other mop-up devices, sufficient detergent-dispersed oil remains in the water to do great harm.

As with the *Amoco Cadiz* spill, the IXTOC I spill, and even the Gulf War disaster, after five years, only a concerted effort could show that a spill had ever happened. After ten years, unless you knew about the spill, you probably could find no evidence at all.

Even ten years after the *Exxon Valdez* spill, I could find only one news reporter willing to tell the truth about it. On Sunday, March 14, 1999, Eric Nalder wrote for the *Seattle Times* an accurate rendition of what happened and the role Captain Hazelwood played. While there may be other truthful articles somewhere, they are well buried. Over and over again one reads about 1,300 miles of ruined beaches, a drunken captain, the largest manmade disaster in history, ad nauseam. Spin has replaced historical fact. Fiction has conquered truth.

Why? The news media reaction was knee jerk as always—this requires no astute insight. It is far more dramatic to thunder about 1,300 miles of polluted coastline than it is to explain that the environmental damage was really fairly slight and that the "good guys" caused at least as much damage as the evil polluters. On the other hand, the environmental groups who so cold bloodedly attacked Exxon and Captain Hazelwood may have been following an agenda that was established well before the Prince William Sound spill.

On Being Green

"It's not easy being green," crooned Kermit the Muppet to an entire generation of tykes. Columnist Alston Chase quoted a German Green politician who had been recently elected to the *Bundestag*—the German parliament: "Grass-roots democracy sounded wonderful before we were elected to Parliament. But now we are in power, centralized solutions seem far more effective."

"Green" is an idea whose time has come. It is impossible today to find a politician who will disavow "the environment." From every side of the political spectrum, long-term members and candidate wannabes alike decry radical actions by fringe Greens, while giving lip service to their so-called underlying principles. Does "Green," as *Time* magazine says, merely mean "our stand on the planet is that we support its survival"? Or is there something behind the rhetoric of survival, beyond National Wildlife calendars, beneath Hollywood movie-star environmental protests?

David Brower, who at eighty-eight succumbed to cancer on November 5, 2000, was widely considered to be the "Archdruid" of the American environmental movement. In their 1993 book *Trashing the Economy*, Ron Arnold and Alan Gottlieb quote Brower: "I founded Friends of the Earth to make the Sierra Club look reasonable. Then I founded Earth Island Institute to make Friends of the Earth look reasonable. Earth First! now makes us look reasonable. We're still waiting for someone to come along and make Earth First! look reasonable." (Earth First! is the group responsible for spiking trees, sabotaging logging equipment, and undertaking other terrorist activities in the name of the environment.)

Brower was arguably the most influential of the environmental activists. He set the tone for the international Green movement: strident and extreme. In her 1990 book *Trashing the Planet*, the late Dixy Lee Ray quotes Brower: "Childbearing [should be] a punishable crime against society, unless the parents hold a government license. . . . All potential parents [should be] required to use contraceptive chemicals, the government issuing antidotes to citizens chosen for childbearing." Catherine Foster writing in *The Christian Science Monitor* on April 8, 1991, quotes Brower: "More is a four letter word. . . . I'd like to declare open season on developers. Not kill them, just tranquilize them." Dixy Lee Ray quotes his mantra in 1993 in her book *Environmental Overkill:* "While the death of young men in war is unfortunate, it is no more serious than the touching of mountains and wilderness areas by humankind."

Wendell Berry, an eloquent agrarian admired by Greens, writes: "In living in the world by his own will and skill, the stupidest peasant or tribesman is more competent than the most intelligent workers or technicians or intellectuals in a society of specialists." Stephanie Mills, the Green journalist, puts it this way: "[Recreation activities of young moderns] may not cultivate the endurance necessary for the kind of labor required to dismantle industrial society and restore the Earth's productivity." Elsewhere she writes, "The ecofascist in me finds it hard to trust even the outcome of a democratic process." She goes on to imply that the only way to save the Earth is for an elite group of biology-smart ecologists to rule the rest of us with benevolent firmness. She concludes that a major element in bringing this about is totally abolishing private ownership of land.

Is this beginning to sound familiar?

The Green Agenda

The Greens are a loosely knit group of people that is being led by a smaller cadre of ideologues who learned social science from Marx and physical science from popular science writers. On this shaky foundation they have built an anti-freedom, anti-democratic, anti-science worldview.

From Marx they learned about the collective, the dialectic, and centralized control, without understanding the lessons from current history following the breakup of the Soviet Union and the worldwide collapse of Communism. From the life sciences they learned about a connection between chemicals and cancer, without understanding the nature of minute dangers and minuscule concentrations or how they translate from the researcher's micro world to the macro world in which we live. From physics and the highly nonintuitive implications of relativity and quantum mechanics they learned that reality is not always what it seems to be. With the help of several misguided physicists, they drew misinformed analogues to Eastern mysticism, connections that reinforced their radically subjective and intuitive (contrasted with experimental and scientific) approach to deep ecology. From a marriage of Marxist theory with a misunderstanding of the second law of thermodynamics, which states that the total energy in the universe never increases, they developed a political-economic system that incorporates no private land ownership and the principle of never expending energy. From a misapplication of quantum physics they derived a new world order that denies the cause and effect of market economics. From scientist ecologists they gained a superficial understanding of the oneness of global processes and the living Earth. Out of metaphor they created reality. The living Earth became a goddess.

The common thread within the Green movement is "stasis," or "sustainability" in their jargon. Their Earth doesn't change; it shows little or no effect from human activity. They want to destroy human infrastructure—our markets, our cities, our communication networks, the very essence that makes us human. They propose to limit human movement by curtailing modern communication methods and transportation. According to Green prophet E. F. Schumacher, the ideal world is where people are "relatively immobile . . . [where] the movement of populations, except in periods of disaster, [is] confined to persons [with] a very special reason to move, such as . . . scholars." In short, it is a place where only the intellectual elite—the eco-bosses—can move about.

Theirs is a simple world. People would not need to understand anything more complex than a shovel or a horse-pulled plow. According to them, if the world is sufficiently simple, ordinary people can understand it in its entirety, and with this understanding comes contentment. Failing this, if the world is sufficiently subjective, ordinary people will be unable to understand it. In the first case, there will be no complexities like nuclear power or space exploration. The ordinary citizen can instead be concerned about how much flour to make, or not tracking horse manure into the house. In the second, ordinary people can be duped by earnest leaders of the eco-movement into opposing things they don't understand until stasis is reached.

Not one new nuclear power plant has been ordered

in the United States since 1979. States like California and Nevada are experiencing severe power shortages. Cut back, citizens are told; cut back on power consumption. Echoing position papers authored by Green activists, our leaders are urging conservation. There is nothing wrong with conservation, but conserving the resources we already have does not solve anything. The only way we can avoid a power outage on a cataclysmic scale is to find and develop new energy sources. Conservation simply will not cut it. Yet that is the preferred solution. And so we inch ever closer to stasis, and the end of progress.

David M. Graber is a research biologist for the National Park Service. He wrote in the *Los Angeles Times* that humans have become a plague upon the Earth, and he suggested that unless Homo sapiens rejoin nature, "some of us can only hope for the right virus to come along." Graber's implications are astonishing. To take his statements seriously is naive, of course. In George Orwell's words: "You have to be an intellectual to believe such nonsense. No ordinary man could be such a fool." Nevertheless, it is only a short step from wishing for the appearance of the right virus to creating and distributing one. A relatively small amount of anthrax virus in the Los Angeles water system would kill the entire population of Southern California.

I have had personal experience in dealing with avowed Greens, in the field during direct confrontations with members of Greenpeace in the high Arctic and down south on the Antarctic continent, and in committee in the Pacific Northwest. There is no way that these people have the collective ability to pull off a widespread conspiracy such as is implied in many of the above quotes. Often, in fact, their leaders have difficulty relating their immediate experiences to objective reality. Here are six cases in point.

The Five-Minute Pirate

In 1982 while I was in Boulder, Colorado, being debriefed following a year at the South Pole, I attended a meeting of Denver Scuba divers. The guest speaker was the then area coordinator for Greenpeace. Between one and two hundred sport divers and other interested individuals attended the weeknight meeting, dressed in business and casual business attire. For the most part these were people who were moderately well off, with a higher than average interest in maintaining the environment. The speaker arrived unwashed, unkempt, and badly needing a change of clothing. The audience politely listened to his story of how he chained himself to the handrail of a Russian whaling ship in a Peruvian port. He said he did this in order to prevent its departure on the next leg of an extended whaling voyage. He was arrested by Peruvian authorities and charged with piracy. It turned out that Peru had no anti-piracy laws, and the Greenpeace member was released. The total cost to Greenpeace for the venture was $30,000. One of the attendees stood after the presentation to ask how long he had delayed the ship's departure. The answer: five minutes.

Dogging NOAA

While working with the National Oceanic and Atmospheric Administration, I was assigned in the late 1970s to the Outer Continental Shelf Environmental Assessment Program to help determine an environmental baseline against which future environmental impacts could be measured. This kind of study is crucial to a complete understanding of the Arctic and should have been high on the Greens' list of good things to do.

Greenpeace dogged us every step of the way, placing

their inflatable outboard boats in the path of our research vessel, forcing us to turn towards icebergs in an obvious attempt to sink us. We never did figure out why they were so opposed to our presence. Perhaps they thought we were a whaling ship—although the letters *NOAA* were prominently displayed on our bow. We were, after all, the "good guys."

McMurdo Shenanigans

While I was at McMurdo Station on the Antarctic continent during the austral summer of 1981 and 1982, Greenpeace showed up with video cameras. Their obvious intent was to capture footage of the terrible environmental damage done to the pristine Antarctic landscape by the evil U.S. Navy polluters. What they discovered, however, were neatly stacked fifty-five-gallon oil drums awaiting transport back to the United States. In fact, the area was a poster-child example of how to manage the environment effectively.

As a precaution, base commander Navy Captain Schoomaker assigned a photographer's mate to tag along with the Greenpeace group. When the Greens could find no obvious polluting activities, they brazenly tipped over the stacks of oil drums, deliberately spilling fuel oil all around the area. They were hoping then to record what they would claim was wanton disregard of the environment by the navy. As it turned out, the most interesting record of that afternoon was made by the photographer's mate, who captured their misdeeds on film.

Antarctic Nuclear Madness

The mindset of Green deep ecology would be amusing

if its consequences were not so drastic. For example, when the U.S. Navy first established its modern year-round operation at McMurdo Station in Antarctica, to supply power, officials initially installed a nuclear reactor of the same type used in U.S. nuclear submarines. These small Westinghouse plants have a perfect safety record. The installed unit should have been able to meet station power requirements indefinitely, with absolutely zero environmental impact. Worldwide condemnation, spearheaded by the Greens, of this U.S. introduction of nuclear power into Antarctica eventually led to shutdown and removal of the reactor. It was replaced by an oil-fired plant that, in the ensuing years, has severely and irretrievably polluted over one hundred thousand square miles of this pristine landscape.

The RTG Fiasco

A radioisotope thermoelectric generator, RTG for short, is a small, very long lasting power source—an outgrowth of the nuclear power program. About the size of a thermos bottle, it can supply useful power for very long periods of time. Because it has no moving parts, it is more reliable than most other power sources, and because it is not dependent upon any outside element, it can supply power where nothing else will work.

RTGs are incredibly simple and safe. Certain substances are naturally radioactive—the atoms of these substances spontaneously change from time to time into simpler substances. When these changes happen, one or more relatively high energy neutrons are released. Because of their high energy, these neutrons can be harmful to living matter, just as bullets or forcefully thrown rocks can be. This natural process of atomic change is called radioactive decay.

One group of substances generates an especially large number of neutrons during this decay process—plutonium and some of its oxides. This is why plutonium is used in nuclear explosives. When a sufficiently large amount of plutonium is concentrated in a special way, neutrons can be forced into a very rapid chain reaction where each neutron creates more neutrons, so that in a fraction of a second incredibly high energies are produced.

Under normal circumstances this cannot happen. In an RTG, a small amount of plutonium dioxide (essentially plutonium rust), far less than the critical mass for a bomb or even that needed to sustain a reactor, is placed inside a container designed to trap the emitted neutrons as heat. With the plutonium, a simple electrical device having no moving parts, called a thermocouple, produces electricity when it gets warm. Since the plutonium can produce heat for a hundred years or more, RTGs can produce electricity that long.

RTGs are especially useful in deep space probes. Solar power could be used, of course, but the collector panels are less efficient, are subject to damage from external sources, and only work well near the sun.

In the mid-1990s, several "environmental" groups expressed serious opposition to using RTGs in space. They publicly decried the "dangers" of nuclear energy, and they insisted on keeping space free of such "dangers." On one hand they seemed to know nothing of the true nature of the space environment: the sun is a continuously exploding hydrogen bomb millions of times the size of the whole Earth; our solar system is filled with high-energy particles, neutrons, cosmic rays—at times it is like the inside of a nuclear reactor. Nothing humans could ever do would have the slightest effect on this environment.

On the other hand, they seemed equally ignorant of the benign character of RTGs. The only possible risk from RTGs could be scattering the thimbleful or so of plutonium into the atmosphere. This is a non-problem for two reasons: RTGs are designed to withstand an uncontrolled return through Earth's atmosphere without breaking up; and even if one did break up, the amount of plutonium is so small that it is extremely unlikely it could even be detected, let alone harm anybody.

The irony is that the focus of ULYSSES, the European Space Agency space probe these groups were objecting to, was solar variability and its effect on Earth's atmosphere, most notably the greenhouse effect. This is a crucial concern to everyone on Earth and a special interest to many environmental groups, including those protesting.

Once again, in October 1997, anti-nuclear groups tried to prevent the "contamination of space with nuclear energy," this time objecting to the launching of the Saturn-bound CASSINI spacecraft. Scheduled for launch on October 6, 1997, CASSINI was powered by three medium-sized RTGs. Since this $3.4 billion spacecraft was scheduled to travel near Saturn, almost a billion miles from the sun, RTG power was unequivocally the best choice for this craft. Following its arrival in the vicinity of Saturn in 2004, CASSINI would study Saturn and its satellites for at least four years and parachute a small probe dubbed HUYGENS onto the surface of Saturn's largest moon, Titan. It was the twenty-fourth U.S. space mission to carry RTGs—including the manned Apollo lunar landings.

The problem here is not the twenty-three eminently successful prior RTG-powered missions, nor the CASSINI mission, but the incredible ignorance demonstrated by the leadership of the anti-nuclear environmental coalition that continues to resist these launches. Their legal interference in the launch of ULYSSES delayed its deployment and nearly doubled its cost. The same kind of legal mischief prior to CASSINI's launch in 1997 delayed that launch by about one and a half weeks.

In a free society, even uninformed people have the right to express their opinions. The leaders of the anti-nuclear environmental coalition have failed to educate themselves even to the most rudimentary level of knowledge regarding RTGs and the space environment. Fortunately, the courts recognized this failure in finding for NASA and the government. Unfortunately, the courts did not place responsibility for the financial cost of the proceedings and the subsequent launch delays where it belonged: Greenpeace, a coalition of Green parties, and other environmental groups.

Power to the Snail Darter and Suckerfish

Fourteen hundred Oregon family farmers located on 200,000 acres in the Klamath Basin are seeing their land dry up and blow away. Yielding to pressure by the Oregon Natural Resources Council, who threatened a lawsuit under the Endangered Species Act, the U.S. Bureau of Reclamation stopped the irrigation water the farmers have used since 1909. The Oregon Natural Resources Council claimed that a small suckerfish currently on the endangered species list would be harmed if the level of the Upper Klamath Lake were reduced. They also cited a need to support the coho salmon run, which, they claimed, also needed the higher water levels.

Remember the snail darter in the Tennessee Valley? Following a public announcement of the little fish's apparent demise, there was a worldwide, Green-driven lament. But when the snail darter turned up in significant numbers in other parts of the country, the silence was deafening. In this case, the suckerfish may be in short supply in Upper Klamath Lake, but it exists far and wide elsewhere. Frankly, even if it were not alive and well—so what? The welfare of 1,400 farmers and their families, and the value of what they produce to the whole nation, far outweighs any possible value of a small fish that plays no role in anything that matters. And the coho salmon run? The 2001 and 2003 runs were two of the largest ever recorded . . . so why even bring it up?

The Endangered Species Act allows any citizen to stop any project anywhere by simply making unsubstantiated claims in a court that is willing to listen. At the time of this writing, only California and Nevada are experiencing severe power shortages. If the Greens go unchecked, however, there are forty-eight states to go. Germany has now given up on nuclear power under pressure from a Green coalition government. It plans to dismantle its plants. France, the world leader in percentage of electricity generated by nuclear power, has stopped building new nuclear plants.

The Greens have lobbied hard for implementation of renewable energy sources such as solar and wind energy. The world's largest power windmill farm is being constructed on the windy heights overlooking the Columbia River Gorge. It is arguably the most environmentally friendly power project ever attempted. Ironically, it is under court challenge—by the Greens.

It seems that the windmill farm threatens an "endangered" condor species . . . go figure.

It really is unlikely that these buffoons will be able to carry out even one of their silly schemes to reorganize and socialize worldwide democracies. What is more probable is that by shouting loud enough for long enough, and gumming up the works while lining the pockets of greedy attorneys, the Greens will lead us to their dream of stasis by default.

CHAPTER 2

The Greenhouse Effect, Ozone Hole, and Other Acorns

Do you remember the story of Chicken Little? Chicken Little was hit on the head by an unseen falling acorn and convinced everyone that the sky was falling. This is a chapter about acorns, big ones and little ones. Some of these acorns relate to other acorns, perhaps because they fell together or close to each other. Some are lone acorns. A couple may even become oak trees, holding up the sky so it won't fall.

The Global Greenhouse

Everybody understands how a backyard greenhouse works. Sunlight shines through the glass and gets trapped inside as heat. Even on a cold winter day, the inside of a greenhouse will be warm and cozy. In fact, if you do not block some of the incoming light, it can actually get too hot. This is why one often sees white-wash on the window panes of a greenhouse. Some of the incoming light is reflected from the painted windows, and so less energy enters the greenhouse and it doesn't get quite as hot.

The Earth is a greenhouse. Our atmosphere is quite transparent to sunlight, except for ultraviolet rays, which are absorbed in the upper atmosphere to form the ozone layer. Light reaching the surface generally is reflected or reradiated as infrared energy—what you feel radiating from a warm pavement. The atmosphere is less transparent to infrared than to visible light, so it retains much of this reflected energy. Just like in the backyard greenhouse, incoming energy is trapped in the planetary greenhouse.

Two atmospheric gases are especially opaque to infrared: carbon dioxide and water vapor. Their presence in significant quantities can dramatically affect global temperature. Other gases can have an effect—methane is a good example (if you raise cows you know what I mean)—but the main ones are carbon dioxide and water vapor.

Carbon dioxide is the result of combustion. It is emitted whether you burn leaves, run an engine, or simply live and breathe. Wildfires are the largest natural source of carbon dioxide, although volcanoes and forests contribute measurably. You probably learned in school that trees absorb carbon dioxide and give off oxygen. During the day this is true, but at night many trees give off carbon dioxide. Generating electricity by burning coal, oil, or gas is the largest manmade source of this gas, with automobiles a distant second. Other sources of carbon dioxide such as fireplaces and barbecues don't count.

Water vapor in the atmosphere is always present. The amount depends upon air temperature—the higher the temperature, the more water vapor. We are not talking about clouds here. Clouds consist of specks of dust surrounded by water droplets. Water vapor is a colorless, odorless gas that makes up a measurable percentage of the atmosphere. We experience this gas as humidity.

In the backyard greenhouse, the only way to increase the internal temperature is to find a way to retain more of the sun's energy that comes through the glass in the first place. Insulate the building. Use a different glass that lets more energy in and then doesn't let it back out. In our planetary greenhouse, this happens when the amount of carbon dioxide in the atmosphere goes up.

Carbon dioxide in our atmosphere has increased due to man's activities from as far back as scientists can measure. In recent times the increase has reached multiple exponential rates. It is not difficult to figure out why. With industrialization, our output of carbon dioxide has increased dramatically. Nearly every industrial activity involves the emission of carbon dioxide, either directly, or indirectly through consumption of electricity, since most common ways of generating electric power release carbon dioxide.

Researchers have created several mathematical models of our atmosphere. Since the 1970s, they have refined these models so that they have become increasingly predictive. None of these is entirely accurate, but all allow relatively accurate predictions for specific phenomena. All clearly predict global temperature increases from increased atmospheric carbon dioxide, although each gives somewhat different results.

It is quite difficult to measure global changes in temperature. Our planetary atmosphere is a very large dynamic system. Trying to establish an average increase of a fraction of a degree is a nearly impossible task. A five-degree temperature increase would be easy to measure, but the thinking is that a change this large would have such cataclysmic effect that we really would like to know what is happening before it goes this far.

One thing is very clear. As the atmosphere warms, it will hold more water vapor, which directly contributes to the warming process. Each of the models predicts a point where global warming increases uncontrollably—like a snowball rolling downhill. Increasing water vapor causes global temperature to increase dramatically and rapidly, once the trigger point is passed. Since none of the models accurately predicts this point, we cannot know how much carbon dioxide and water vapor will trigger this effect. It is clear, nevertheless, that once the effect is triggered, once global temperature begins to spiral upwards uncontrollably, there is nothing humankind can do to stop it—at least nothing we know about today.

Oceanic models predict sufficient melting of polar ice when this happens to raise worldwide sea levels by as much as twenty feet. A glance at any globe will make it clear what kind of disaster would result from this.

But wait a minute. Remember the backyard greenhouse? Remember the whitewashed panes? Let's go back to the model; let's take another look at the predictions. There doesn't seem to be any question that an increase in greenhouse gases—primarily carbon dioxide—will cause the atmospheric temperature to increase. In fact, the reason we have relatively balmy temperatures around the world, on average anyway, is because we are currently experiencing a stabilized planetary greenhouse. Let's buy into the models that predict an increase in temperature. We won't worry about how much. This increase, no matter how large or small, will produce a corresponding increase in atmospheric water vapor—more for some models and less for others, but always an increase. This additional water vapor increases the greenhouse effect, which increases the temperature, which increases the water vapor, which . . .

But wait. What happens when the humidity goes up in the late afternoon on a sweltering day? Remember those thunderheads you loved to watch as a child? At some point, and this is not very well understood, atmospheric water vapor changes to clouds, and clouds block incoming sunlight. We have models for this as well. These models predict that if you generate sufficient cloud cover, it doesn't really matter how warm the atmosphere gets—it will cool rapidly. Depending on circumstances, this can carry the planet right into a massive ice age. Now understand that these models are just as predictive as the models leading to runaway high temperatures.

What we do not have yet is a way to connect these models into a whole system. It is not a matter of what you believe, or what you would like to see. Both sets of models are right; they all make accurate predictions. It's just that we have no idea at all how to get from here to there. We simply do not know what will happen when a runaway atmospheric greenhouse takes over. It could get very hot. It could get very cold. The effects could cancel each other out, leaving us about where we are now. We could experience short-term wild temperature swings.

The point is that we simply do not know.

The upward spiral of atmospheric carbon dioxide has been going on for a long time. Yes, it is accelerating, but all the models agree that, whatever happens, it will not happen overnight, or in a week, or in a month. Time is on our side. We have time to figure out what is really likely to happen. We have time to come to grips with the situation. We do know that the principal source of carbon dioxide is the production of electricity by burning fossil fuel. We also know that whatever happens, the trigger will be some level of atmospheric carbon dioxide greater than what we have today. It seems prudent, therefore, that we cut back on carbon dioxide production when practical.

From the mid-1950s to the mid-1960s, most new power plants were nuclear. During this period, the global increase of carbon dioxide was nearly halted. With the onset of worldwide movements (except for in France and the Soviet Union) to limit nuclear power plants, carbon dioxide production resumed dramatically.

One solution to this potentially huge problem is

obvious. Until we develop efficient alternative energy sources, we really should be putting a great deal of emphasis on tried and tested nuclear power.

The sky is not falling here, folks. We will neither fry nor freeze tomorrow, and maybe nothing at all will ever happen. It does seem kind of silly, though, to burn oil, coal, and gas when they could be used as raw material for so many other things we need, especially since we really do have a very safe, efficient, renewable way to generate electricity.

The Great Ozone-Hole Hoax

The Greens have "alerted" all of us to the alarming possibility that we are destroying the Earth's ozone layer and threatening all life on Earth.

It's an interesting premise. Let's examine this acorn more closely.

Ozone is an unstable molecule formed when free oxygen atoms are released in an oxygen-rich atmosphere. That fresh smell following a thunderstorm is the ozone created by the electric bolts we call lightning. O_3—ozone—is a molecule consisting of three oxygen atoms, unlike O_2—oxygen—which consists of two oxygen atoms. Free oxygen atoms cannot exist by themselves. They immediately combine to form O_2, oxygen. When free atoms of oxygen are released in an oxygen atmosphere, one of two things happens: they either combine with each other to form more O_2, or they combine with O_2 to form O_3—ozone. Because ozone is naturally unstable, over time it will decay, losing one of the oxygen atoms. The free oxygen atoms so formed combine with themselves to form O_2.

In our atmosphere, most ozone is created when normal oxygen molecules are split apart near the top of the atmosphere by the action of ultraviolet light in normal sunshine. In the process, the ultraviolet is absorbed, so that it never reaches the Earth's surface—hence the "protection" that the ozone layer is said to provide to our planet. Of course, this occurs near the top of the atmosphere, where the ultraviolet first encounters the oxygen. Strictly speaking, therefore, it is not ozone that forms a protective layer, but rather ozone is formed as a consequence of the "protective" process, where O_2 splits into oxygen atoms while absorbing the ultraviolet. Of course, all the ozone that is created also absorbs ultraviolet—hence the "protective ozone layer."

As mentioned earlier, ozone decays naturally. It is broken apart faster in the presence of CFCs (refrigerants and propellants), oxides of nitrogen (auto emissions, power plants, forest fires, and volcanoes), and methane (agriculture and volcanoes). The chemistry is a bit complicated, but the bottom line is that when these gases are present and mix with ozone, more of the ozone decays than when these gases are not present. Thus, ozone that drifts into the lower atmosphere tends to be destroyed. The opposite is also true. When these gases drift into the upper atmosphere, they increase the natural decay rate of the ozone.

When ozone molecules break up spontaneously at the top of the atmosphere, new ozone is created immediately by the sun's ultraviolet light. Studies on how long this process takes indicate that ozone regenerates fast enough to preclude significant ultraviolet effects at the Earth's surface. Put another way, when a ray of ultraviolet sunlight manages to slip past the initial clumping of ozone, because an O_3 molecule happens not to be there, it runs smack into a regular old oxygen molecule and splits it apart, getting absorbed in the process and, by the way, generating replacement ozone.

This process is not an absolute. Some ultraviolet

always reaches the Earth's surface. Since the thickness of the ozone varies continuously, the amount of ultraviolet at any spot on the Earth's surface also changes continuously, not to mention the effects of clouds, water vapor, smog, etc.

The Earth is tilted 23.5 degrees to the ecliptic, which means that the Earth's axis forms a 23.5 degree angle to the plane formed by the Earth's orbit around the sun. As the Earth moves along its orbital path, at midsummer in the Northern Hemisphere the North Pole is tilted to its maximum towards the sun. Six months later it is tilted to its maximum away from the sun. In between, the tilt is parallel. What this means at the poles is that the sun never sets in the summer; it just goes around and around the horizon, reaching a height of 23.5 degrees at midsummer. At the autumnal equinox, the sun rolls on the horizon, and then it begins to move below the horizon, until it reaches a maximum amount of 23.5 degrees below at midwinter. It then ascends again, reaching the horizon at spring equinox, and repeats the cycle. In simple terms, this amounts to three months of direct sunlight, three months of twilight, three months of darkness, and three more months of twilight. Remember what happens to ozone when it is left by itself: it decays away; it becomes plain oxygen.

So let's put this acorn together.

For three summer months at the poles, the sun's ultraviolet light generates and maintains a distinct ozone layer atop the Earth's oxygen atmosphere. Then follow nine months of twilight and night and twilight again, during which—as they say—the "sun don't shine." But the ozone continues to decay . . . so guess what? The "ozone layer" gets really thin up there. A thinning of the ozone layer—a "hole"—appears above the polar region. It always has and always will.

The "hole" is an artifact of the polar night. The effect

is enhanced by the presence of CFCs, nitrogen oxides, and methane, but it is not caused by these agents.

Buildup of CFCs, nitrogen oxides, and methane may inevitably result in an overall thinning of the ozone layer, but the amount of these substances that would cause immediate dissolution of each ozone molecule the moment it forms would wreak direct havoc on our atmosphere long before it would totally prevent the formation of an ozone layer. Ozone-layer thinning caused by "normal industrial amounts" of CFCs will be insignificant, especially when compared to the effects of volcanic eruptions combined with summer methane production from Northern Hemisphere agriculture (you know—cows!).

Prof. S. Fred Singer, who is on leave from the University of Virginia, directs the Washington-based Science & Environmental Policy Project. He recently served as chief scientist of the Department of Transportation and earlier as the first director of the U.S. Weather Satellite Program. Some of his scientific accomplishments relate to the ozone issue. He devised the ozone monitor used in satellites and was the first to publish on ozone destruction by anthropogenic methane. Dr. Singer has written extensively on the ozone issue for both professional and popular audiences. He points out several times that if one were to take the worst-case scenario for ozone depletion and subsequent increase in ultraviolet activity at the Earth's surface, it would produce a total change in ultraviolet levels roughly equivalent to moving from New York City to Miami.

It was the austral summer, 1981. I was at the geographic South Pole—Amundson-Scott Station, they call it. I was in charge of South Polar atmospheric monitoring for the National Science Foundation and the National Oceanic and Atmospheric Administration under the auspices of GMCC—Geophysical Monitoring for Climate Change. Part of my duties was to measure the ozone layer from the surface using a Dobson Meter, a device that generates a relative measure of the thickness of the ozone at the top of the atmosphere. During this period, I was able to coordinate my measurements with measurements made simultaneously from the *Nimbus 7* polar-orbiting satellite. For the first time in history, we were able to establish an absolute measure of the ozone-layer thickness. This was pretty heady stuff.

During the summer, Amundson-Scott Station has a relatively high number of visitors. Among others, we hosted a group of senators and their assistants, and a group of news people. One of these was Dale Van Atta, who was there representing Pulitzer Prize winner and investigative reporter Jack Anderson. Dale came out to my lab looking for something out of the ordinary. In my capacity as a uniformed officer with NOAA, I did not want to contribute directly to his mischief, but I did tell him about our ozone measuring success. I also pointed him towards a female scientist working at McMurdo Station. This lady was especially attractive, and I had learned during a visit there that she was hugely upset that the 1,000 male occupants of the station insisted on viewing her as a female instead of a scientist. I thought she might have a thing or two to say to Dale Van Atta.

It turned out that essentially everyone in Antarctica had heard about our linking the ground and satellite measurements of the ozone thinning. In other words, the hole was no longer just hypothetical—we had actually established its existence. As I said, it was pretty heady stuff. It was this acorn that the lady scientist chose to drop on Mr. Van Atta. Apparently, she painted a dramatic picture for him of ultraviolet poisoning, widespread environmental damage, and massive human cancers. And sure enough, shortly after he returned to the United States, the story broke in the *New York Times.*

In reaction, Congress passed legislation financing massive new atmospheric research. For the first time in their professional lives, atmospheric scientists had sufficient funds. These guys weren't stupid. They used the money well. And when the furor began to die down, NASA sent a plane into the high Arctic during the polar spring, and guess what they found: another hole. Acorns were falling everywhere. And, of course, Congress appropriated more money.

I should add that along with the money, under pressure from the Greens and their sympathizers, Congress legislated a phaseout of CFCs and certain other chemicals that were thought to be the root cause of the first hole. With the "discovery" of the other hole in the Arctic, Congress accelerated this phaseout, to the delight of those same forces and, of course, the commercial interests who benefited from the phase-in of the replacement technologies and chemicals.

All good things must end. Eventually, in the late 1990s, NASA announced that recent research had produced a surprising result: the ozone layer was repairing itself much more quickly than had been expected. The picnic was over.

But from the acorn grew a mighty oak that reached to the sky.

Acid Rain

A country vocalist croons that we "burn fossil fuel and get it back as acid rain." A popular conception is that many of our forests are being depleted to manufacture paper and that the remainder are dying because of acid rain; that our lakes are becoming acid laden, killing fish and other aquatic life. This is based in large part on the mineral titration theory, which was the key to environmentalist alarms regarding the acid rain threat during the 1980s. As quoted by Chetly Zarko in a 1992 article in *The Michigan Review*, William Anderson, professor of economics at the University of Tennessee, succinctly summarized mineral titration theory. This theory asserted that acidic soils "have little buffering capacity against acid rain. Because much of the soil in the Northeast and eastern Canada is acidic, many scientists simply assumed that acid rain ran off directly into streams and lakes and made them acidic. . . . Scientific models based on the mineral titration theory predict that eliminating half of the acidity of rain could raise the pH level to a more neutral and life-supporting" level over fifty years. The mineral titration theory also predicted that the sulfur dioxide in acid rain was destroying forests by stripping soil of nutrients, eroding tree bark, and leaching soil metals into the groundwater.

In order to assess this potentially devastating problem, in 1980 Congress created and funded the National Acid Precipitation Assessment Program (NAPAP). Seven hundred leading environmental scientists participated in NAPAP research, spending $540 million to define the problem, establish its extent, and develop solutions.

After ten years, these eminent researchers reached several startling conclusions. The late Warren T. Brookes, the renowned, hard-hitting economics columnist, summarized the results in *The Quill*, and the late Dixy Lee Ray, scientist, Washington governor, and ecological gadfly, wrote about them in her best-selling book *Environmental Overkill*.

Forests aren't dying—they're expanding. For example, in 1952, U.S. forestland consisted of 664 million acres containing 610 billion cubic feet of growing stock. In 1987, this had increased by 10 percent and

24 percent respectively, to 728 million acres with 756 billion cubic feet. Most of this increase has been on private land in the Northeast and South.

Acid rain seems to affect only a relatively small number of red spruce growing high in the northern Appalachians, but the evidence is ambiguous—the acidic level of the rain may not be the problem at all. It seems that these trees are under environmental duress because of conditions where they grow—primarily wind and cold. Furthermore, throughout the Northeast, many species of trees and bushes actually thrive in acidic soil. Red and black spruce, eastern hemlock, balsam fir, oaks, rhododendrons, and blueberries prefer acidic soil. The nitrogen and sulfur contained in rain that falls in these areas actually fertilizes some three hundred million acres on which it falls. Crop yields and protein counts in these areas are up significantly as a result of the acid rain. This has not been reported by the media in the United States, although the same result figures prominently in a Swedish report on the same subject as reported by Edward Krug in a 1991 article in the *Cleveland Plain Dealer.*

The best available information, taken from a review of Indian history and the evidence of lake-bottom core samples, shows that those lakes were acidic and fishless before the 1800s. Dr. Edward Krug, who led the original NAPAP study, says the Iroquois word "Adirondack" means "bark eater." According to Zarko, Anderson says that lake fish populations at the turn of the last century thrived due to "extensive slash-and-burn logging. Eliminating the acid vegetation caused the soil to become more alkaline [a high pH], reducing the acid flowing into lakes and streams. In turn, the lakes became more hospitable to fish. After 'forever wild' legislation stopped the logging in 1915, the watersheds reverted to acid soils and vegetation, and the lakes became acidic again." NAPAP measured the highest acid-rain level in the Ohio Valley—but found no acid lakes there at all. Florida, New Zealand, and Australian lakes all are more acidic than Adirondack lakes, even though their soil is similar and they have essentially no acid rain. In fact, the most significantly acidic lakes were found in Florida.

The information contained in this report should have been welcome news for every concerned citizen. Although these results were widely accepted by the scientific community, unfortunately, the information was not acceptable either to the Environmental Protection Agency or to the Greens. Environmentalist political pressure on Congress, and action by several members of Congress—including especially Rep. James Scheuer (D-N.Y.), who called the report "intellectually dishonest"—eventually persuaded the EPA to replace the original director of NAPAP, Dr. J. Lawrence Kulp, with Dr. James Mahoney, and to fire Krug. According to Brookes in *Consumer Alert Comments,* Dr. Mahoney was then directed to rewrite the report and repudiate its findings.

Science had virtually overturned every tenet of the mineral titration theory. Nevertheless the 1990 amendments to the Clean Air Act ignored this. They mandated pH-balance improvements to seventy-five lakes at an estimated cost of $200 billion over fifty years—$2.7 billion per lake. And they required installation of scrubbers in old power-plant smokestacks to remove 10 million tons of sulfur by the year 2000, costing consumers $5 to $7 billion per year.

Under Kulp, NAPAP had recommended liming selected lake watersheds and mandating a phase-in of "clean coal" technology. The total cost for this proposal, which encompasses every acidic lake in the United States and Canada, is $50 million. There is no additional cost to power consumers, and—in the estimate of these 700 scientists—the entire problem would be solved.

Ironically, when Mahoney was asked what would happen to lake and stream acidity if nothing at all were done over the next fifty years, he replied: "Nothing."

The scrubbing mandated by the Clean Air Act amendments produces three tons of toxic limestone sludge and one ton of carbon dioxide (the major "greenhouse gas") for every ton of sulfur dioxide removed. Brookes predicted that if this act were actually enforced, by 1999 we would have needed landfill space for 30 million tons of this toxic sludge.

The revised NAPAP report was issued in stages during 1990. The encouraging information in the original report was suppressed by environmental concerns, and Congress went on to pass the legislation. Midwest coal-burning power plants were required to install scrubbing equipment, even though the coal immediately available to them was low sulfur and met the EPA requirements without scrubbing. The overall economics made it cheaper for them to purchase high-sulfur coal from the Northeast. A complete pollutant accounting of their situation shows that the overall pollutant level has risen as a result of all this. The only beneficiaries appear to be coal-mining operations in the Northeast and the environmental organizations they generously supported during the lobbying effort in Congress.

Kulp and Krug were eventually redeemed in the EPA's eyes, since they had the backing of essentially the entire scientific community, but the damage had been done. The report was heavily edited and modified to fit the political climate brought about by the environmental lobby and Northeastern mining interests. The amendments to the Clean Air Act were signed by Pres. George Herbert Walker Bush before the report's release. These amendments contained market-based provisions for trading pollution credits. Companies received "credits" that could be "spent" to control pollution, and a firm that did not need all its credits could sell those to a firm that needed more. This provided a cost-effective way of getting private industry to pay for its own cleanup. The first Bush administration was reluctant to tamper with the report and risk losing these provisions in a rewrite.

More recently, in 1996, NAPAP conducted an assessment of costs, benefits, and effectiveness of acid-rain controls. Among other things, this report concluded that "most forest ecosystems are not currently known to be adversely impacted by acid deposition." But under pressure from the Greens, it then dropped a significant acorn: "if deposition levels [of SO2] are not reduced in areas where they are presently high, adverse effects may develop in more forests due to chronic, multiple-decade exposure." This speculative statement is completely unsupported by data in the report.

You can draw your own conclusions about who would benefit more from these programs: we taxpaying citizens who live and work in the environment, or those individuals and organizations responsible for administering the vast sums that you and I pay and those groups who gain from the unholy and politically powerful marriage between tree huggers and Northeast mining interests.

Perhaps Chicken Little knows more about the sky than she lets on.

Celebrating Earth Day

In your mind, travel back to 1970, the year the first Earth Day happened. Flower children loved freely on our college campuses, but emerging violent protest painted an ugly backdrop. Leisure suits were popular, although men wearing them were developing thick waistlines and high foreheads. The micro miniskirt had replaced the mini, and "topless" had migrated from strip joints to certain "in"-crowd parties. Norman Cousins, well-known editor of *Saturday Review*, stated flatly that "the human race is operating under the starkest of deadlines." NBC's Edwin Newman warned that by 1980 the great rivers of this nation "would have reached the boiling point." *Life* predicted that city dwellers would need gas masks by 1980. So did Wisconsin senator Gaylord Nelson (who actually claimed to be the originator of Earth Day). He also predicted that by 1995 "between 75 and 80 percent of all the species of living animals will be extinct." Then he went out on a limb, forecasting that by 2000 the natural environment would be unable to support any life. Other predictions included: by 1974, there would be water rationing and a ban on flush toilets; by the mid-1970s, there would be a 500 percent increase in dysentery (with flush toilets banned!); by 1980, there would be worldwide food rationing.

Dr. Paul Erlich, who wrote the bestseller *The Population Bomb* and founded the organization Zero Population Growth, deserves special mention. Along with his dire predictions, he supplied some interesting solutions. "The time of famines will be upon us full scale in 1975," he told Johnny Carson. Smog masks, synthetic steaks, maximal regimentation and government control . . . his list of dire problems is nearly endless. He predicted a "tremendous impact" from Earth Day in 1970, saying it "is going to generate a lot of civil disobedience . . . people are just going to stop paying their bills." He also foresaw a new national political party emerging out of Zero Population Growth. (President Erlich?)

His solutions to these overwhelming problems are enlightening. He called for a federal Department of Population and Environment, a head tax for families with children, lots of abortions, an end to "death-control" (meaning life-extension medical research), and compulsory birth regulation. "We might, for instance," he proposed, "institute a system whereby a temporary sterilant would be added to a staple food or to the water supply."

Sure, it's silly—all of it. And yet, the people quoted here are not wackos. They are serious journalists, respected writers, honored environmentalists. They are people of stature in our society. What they say matters. So why were they talking such nonsense? Granted, we are examining their silliness through our most excellent hindsight, but in 1970 it really was very unlikely that flush toilets would be banned four years later or that rivers would boil in ten. How can these people say and publish such foolishness, and then ask us to respect their wisdom and judgment afterwards?

Dr. Dixy Lee Ray was my zoology professor at the University of Washington. She was also my friend and mentor. Her accomplishments include: governor of Washington, chairman of the Atomic Energy Commission (precursor to the Department of Energy), assistant secretary of state for oceans, and recipient of the United Nations Peace Prize. In *Environmental Overkill* she wrote: "We believe it is just as wrong to exaggerate the seriousness of environmental issues as it is to downplay the remarkable resilience and recovery powers of nature." She goes on to say that "it's important to demonstrate that a proposed solution [to an environmental problem] is appropriate, practical, and affordable."

There are no acorns here. This is an oak tree I can deal with.

Water, Water, Everywhere . . .

Drought is becoming a way of life for many Southwestern communities. They sing the refrain,

"Water, water, everywhere but here . . . ," as with covetous eyes they gaze at the Columbia River and its tributaries. Several are seriously proposing to divert some of this water southwards.

The Columbia is a great river. Most of its water flows into the sea, so what difference will it make to divert some?

Their arguments are well thought out and persuasive.

Naturally, the people who depend upon this water for their existence have raised serious objections. Some of these look to future water needs in the Northwest, pointing out that the time is coming when the Northwest will need all the water it can get. Since people who take the long view are routinely ignored, these objections have fallen on deaf ears.

Then Chicken Little gets involved with a host of environmental objections. Some of these fall into the same category as the ones the Greens routinely raise when dams are being contemplated. Others are the same objections that the Chicken Little mentality always raises when any kind of change is proposed. Sometimes they are valid and sometimes not. It goes without saying, however, that any significant diverting of a major river will significantly impact the environment. In a rational society, such effects must be weighed against the benefits—which is why dams get built.

Even if the Greens and the other Chicken Littles don't convince you, you are, nevertheless, unlikely to ignore the cost. To divert a meaningful amount of Columbia River water to drought-stricken regions of the Southwest would cost significantly more than the annual budget of several states. This would be a major, world-class engineering undertaking.

Nobody doubts that these regions need water. Most people would not begrudge their getting water from wherever it is available so long as reasonable criteria are met in the process. With all due respect to the long-termers and the environmental observers, the main criterion here seems to be cost. If we can lick the cost, we're going to do it.

There is a potential solution to this problem that completely bypasses the first objection, that sidesteps the environmental issues (while introducing a new set that is far more benign), and that does not ascend into the financial stratosphere.

Unlike oil and coal, water is cyclically renewable in weeks and months rather than eons. Nearly 90 percent of the world's fresh water supply is tied up in polar ice. Large portions of this are contained in ice blocks called tabular icebergs floating off Antarctica.

What would it take to hook up several oceangoing tugs to one of these bergs and tow it up the coast to Los Angeles? Anchor it, or perhaps ground it firmly, and surround it with a floating rubber curtain that extends about fifteen feet below the surface. Since the ice is fresh water, and since fresh water floats on salt water, Los Angeles can simply pump the fresh water ashore and put it into the water system. Purification, if it is required at all, will be minimal. When the berg shrinks to a predetermined size, we simply go south to get another one.

This system costs more than you might think but very substantially less than the cost of diverting the Columbia. Experts say it will be a cost-effective alternative to (translate this as "able to compete with") conventional water sources within five years.

Problems with solutions don't bother me.

Green Semantics

As we have explored the "Green world" together, you

may have gotten the impression that "environment" and "environmentalist" have very little in common.

You are familiar with the word "ghetto." In today's parlance, a "ghetto" is an area of a modern city inhabited mostly by African-Americans. Actually, this is not at all what "ghetto" means. A ghetto was a place in most European cities during the 1800s where Jews were required to live. The key word here is *required.* Civil rights leaders during the 1960s saw the economic and social isolation of America's blacks as analogous to the legal isolation of Jews in Europe. While nobody can quarrel with the analogy, their use of the word "ghetto" to describe predominantly black areas carries with it the implication that there is legal sanction to the isolation. Since this is not true, in effect they changed the meaning of the word "ghetto." Civil rights leaders wanted to implant an image in the mind of America that equated the historic treatment of European Jewry with the then-current treatment of African-Americans.

It obviously worked. Our language is dynamic— today, "ghetto" means exactly what civil rights leaders wanted it to mean. Unfortunately, it is now impossible to convey to a listener the concept of the original ghetto without adding a lengthy explanation.

Exactly the same thing is happening to the word "environmentalist." It used to describe a person who was professionally concerned with the scientific study of the environment, just as a physicist studies physics and a historian studies history. But it is beginning to describe an extremist political activist whose interest focuses on the environment and whose solutions to perceived problems include significant government involvement and—often—radical measures.

Fortunately, there still are classical environmentalists around. Admittedly, some of these also fit the "new" definition, but many quietly pursue their research in the classic scientific mold.

No rational individual would disagree that healthy change is good for our society. One can even argue for the occasional use of force—after all, America's nationhood started with a revolution. When Earth First members drive steel spikes into trees, however, causing loggers' power saws to shatter with potentially horrendous consequences for individual loggers, they go too far. Our modern society contains elegant mechanisms for bringing about needed change peacefully, without disruption and without ecoterrorism.

The Nature Conservancy (TNC) is an environmental organization that totally understands this principle. TNC works by identifying the species and ecosystems in greatest need of immediate protection and determining areas that should be set aside to ensure their survival; protecting habitats and natural systems through direct land acquisition, by gift or purchase; and managing for the long-term the protection of species and ecosystems on more than fourteen hundred TNC-owned preserves in all fifty states and encouraging compatible use of those sanctuaries by researchers, educators, and the public.

All TNC does is purchase land where there are endangered species or ecosystems—a simple, elegant solution to a complex problem!

TNC has over a million members, including many of the nation's top corporations. Surprise—corporations, and the men and women who run them, care, too! In the United States, since 1951 TNC has purchased or acquired millions of acres of old-growth timber, native grassland, endangered mountain plants, marshland, and white-oak savannah. It currently has a holding of 12,098,000 acres in the United States and 61,750,000 acres internationally.

The Nature Conservancy is a mighty oak that holds up all kinds of sky. It sure beats spiking trees!

CHAPTER 3

The Sun and the Atom:
The Only Sources of Electricity

Only two sources of electricity are available to humans at this stage of our development: solar and atomic.

All Things Solar

When we burn anything to generate electricity, we release solar energy stored as biomass in coal, oil, gas, wood, or even municipal garbage. Dig back to what you learned about chlorophyll in high-school biology or botany or in a general science class you attended somewhere in your past. Unless you pursued a professional career in this area, you probably don't remember a lot about this subject, but you probably do remember that chlorophyll allows a plant to use sunlight. Through photosynthesis, chlorophyll allows plants to capture some of the energy contained in sunlight and to use this energy, combined with water and carbon dioxide, to create sugar and oxygen.

This is the mechanism that generates the oxygen we breathe, although more than half our oxygen comes from single-cell plants floating in the oceans—called phytoplankton. Plant cells then use some of this oxygen and the sugar to generate ATP—adenosine triphosphate—which is the energy coin of the cell, one of the common ways living things store energy. Interestingly, one of the byproducts of this process is carbon dioxide. So when plants take in sunlight, they give off oxygen, and then as they use the energy, they give off carbon dioxide. (When former president Ronald Reagan made his oft-derided remark about redwoods polluting the atmosphere, therefore, he was right.) As plants use their stored energy, they grow, creating cellulose in its many forms. In effect, the energy that originally came from the sun eventually ends up stored in the chemical structure of cellulose and the rest of the plant matter—collectively called biomass.

Biomass can end up almost anywhere. Cover a concentrated amount of biomass with sediment, subject it to great pressure for a long time, and you end up with coal, or perhaps oil. Under certain circumstances either of these can produce natural gas. Coal, oil, and natural gas represent concentrated forms of biomass. When we burn these, the energy we release is the same energy captured from sunlight many eons ago. When we burn wood, we release solar energy captured recently, perhaps even yesterday. When we burn anything else, no matter what it is, it eventually reduces to some form of biomass that got its original shot of energy from the sun. In other words, all of it still is solar energy, at least indirectly.

The sun deposits a great deal of its earthbound energy on the oceans. Much of this energy is reflected off the oceans' surface back to space. Some of the incoming energy is absorbed into the oceans' surface, and some of the reflected energy is absorbed by the atmosphere. We looked at this phenomenon earlier during our discussion of greenhouse gases and how carbon dioxide and water vapor in the atmosphere increase the amount of reflected energy the atmosphere retains. In that discussion we learned how the net effect of this process is increased levels of water vapor in the atmosphere, and ultimately an increase in the cloud layer. Here we will concentrate on the dynamics of the process itself.

The Solar Energy Cycle

Solar energy plays two direct roles: it evaporates water and, by warming the atmosphere, increases its ability to carry more water vapor. Solar energy also plays a significant indirect role. Some places are warmer than others. By a relatively complicated mechanism, these differences in air temperature result in pressure differences. Air located in an area of higher pressure will naturally flow towards areas of lower pressure. The exact path the air takes is a function of many things, including the shape of the land and the rotation of the Earth. The net result, however, is wind. When you think about it, therefore, the motion of the air—the wind— is a form of solar energy.

We can directly recapture solar energy from the wind by placing a windmill in its path. Many Western windy ridges host armies of wind generators. These farms of tall, single-mast, high-tech windmills suck a significant amount of solar energy out of the passing air. The hardware is simple but still relatively fragile. As more and more of these systems come into use, the technology will become increasingly robust.

We have been indirectly recapturing solar energy for millennia using flowing water. Remember all that water vapor that found its way into the atmosphere through the action of solar energy? Much of this water eventually forms into water droplets that make up clouds. Under the right conditions, these droplets coalesce into raindrops that fall to Earth, either back into the ocean to undergo the cycle all over again, or on land somewhere. When they fall, they give up something called potential energy. In effect, each raindrop contains a level of potential energy exactly equivalent to the amount of total solar energy it took to get the raindrop from the ocean where it originated to the point from which it begins to fall. When a raindrop falls into the ocean, it has given up its entire store of potential energy; every bit of solar energy that it took to create the water vapor, coalesce it into a droplet, and transport it to the rain location is gone. When the landing spot is higher than sea level, however, the raindrop sitting on the Earth's surface still contains some potential energy.

So here's the whole story. Melting snowfields, rainstorm runoff, brooks, streams, rivers, lakes—all this massive amount of water eventually finds its way back to the ocean. Sure, some of it evaporates and gets recycled locally, but eventually all of it comes home. Every inch of descent represents a surrender of potential energy.

Hydro Power

Humans have captured this energy in different ways for millennia. The ancient Egyptians placed crude paddlewheels in flowing water and used this power to grind wheat into flour and for other purposes. An obvious improvement to this method is to dam a stream to generate a more powerful flow of water that can turn a larger mill or drive a faster machine.

Hydroelectric dams are a modern example of the indirect use of solar energy. Massive amounts of water are stored behind dams, and the water is then allowed to flow through turbine blades on its way to the next lower level. The turbine blades rotate large generators to produce electricity. The water below the dam is once again accumulated behind another dam, and so on, until insufficient drop remains to produce meaningful power, or until the geography no longer permits further cost-effective accumulation of water.

Even energy extracted from the rising and falling ocean tides ultimately derives at least partly from the sun. Admittedly, this connection is more tenuous, since the moon plays a significant role, and this energy is gravitational instead of solar radiation. This method of power generation exists mainly in experimental setups.

A minor non-solar power source located in certain isolated regions is geothermally generated power. In regions of high geothermal activity, it is possible to harness some of this energy by using pressurized steam or hot water from underground, or by exploiting large temperature differences created by the geothermal activity.

All Things Nuclear

The only significant exception to solar-generated electricity is energy derived by releasing the binding energy of atoms, either as fission when we split heavy atoms like uranium, or as fusion when we combine light atoms like hydrogen. We are expert at the first, but we haven't quite figured out how to accomplish the second.

An examination of atomic power—nuclear energy—cannot be undertaken without a discussion of the twin "problems" of radiation and nuclear waste. First we will tackle radiation. Then, after we develop a good understanding of how nuclear reactors work, what they are and, what they are not, we'll spend some time talking about nuclear waste.

Radiation

Step outside on a nice day and feel the sun's

warmth—that's radiation; so is the light. A body's warmth is radiation. So are radio waves, television signals, X-rays, and light from a glowworm's tail.

Radiation is energy transfer. It can take several forms. One is tiny mass-less packets called photons. We experience photons most commonly as ordinary light. This radiation frequently is called electromagnetic radiation. Photons carry energy, and the more energetic they are—the higher their frequency—the more "dangerous" they can be. Harm results when energy is transferred to living cells in a damaging way. Early atomic scientists identified a form of radiation they called "gamma-rays." Ironically, this radiation turned out to be nothing more than high-energy photons, but the name still is frequently used. So when certain reactions produce high-energy photons, instead of referring to them as "high-energy photons," scientists usually call them "gamma-rays," but they are identical.

In 1895 William Roentgen discovered a form of radiation that has become known as X-rays. Not very long thereafter, scientists determined that X-rays were energetic photons with less energy than gamma-rays but with more energy than ultraviolet light.

In school we all learned about the atomic nucleus surrounded by a cloud of electrons. Most of us probably carry a mental picture of a little solar system with a sun-like nucleus surrounded by electrons representing the planets. Keep this useful analogy in mind as we move forward.

The Pond

Near the beginning of the twentieth century, physicists developed a picture of energy as waves moving through something they called the "ether"—try to envision waves moving across a pond of water. Much of what they observed about the behavior of light and other forms of energy could be explained using this analogy.

If you drop two pebbles into a pond, the two expanding patterns of waves will interact with each other, forming completely predictable and fully understood interference patterns. It turned out that light emanating from two sources behaved in exactly the same manner. Just like the waves in the pond, the light "waves" interfered with each other, creating interference patterns. Indeed, even today the mathematical equations describing this behavior are the best way to deal with electromagnetic energy under certain circumstances.

Back in the pond, if you place an obstacle like a large stone in the path of the advancing waves, several things can happen. If the obstacle is smaller than half the distance between the wave peaks, the waves pass right by the obstacle with little or no interference. Once the obstacle's size increases beyond half the distance between the wave peaks, however, it begins to interfere with the passing waves. Depending on its size, the waves may bend or refract as they pass the obstacle, which can lead to an interference pattern behind the obstacle. As the obstacle gets even larger, eventually the waves striking it will either be reflected or absorbed. If reflected, they will form an interference pattern in front of the obstacle.

During this discussion we have been referring to the size of the obstacle. We could just as well not have changed the obstacle's size and instead changed the distance between wave peaks or, put another way, shortened the frequency of the waves. Remember when you took a bath as a child? You could make waves in the bathtub by moving your hand up and down in the water. If you moved your hand slowly, the waves you generated undulated slowly across the tub, and the distance between the waves was relatively large. If you moved your hand up and down swiftly, in other words if you put a lot of energy into your wave making, the resulting waves were larger, and the distance between them was very short. Waves with shorter wavelengths carry more energy—kind of obvious, really, since more wave fronts pass a point per time interval, and of course, they are higher.

Two things are important here. When the obstacle begins to interfere with the passing waves, some of the energy in the waves actually gets transferred to the obstacle. Until that size relationship exists, nothing happens. Once it exists, you can then increase the amount of energy absorbed by the obstacle either by shortening the wavelength or by increasing the size of the wave peaks, which are two sides of the same coin since they are linked. On the beach of an island in the ocean, this absorbed energy pounds beach rocks into sand. If the waves arrive more often and are larger, there is more pounding. The significant point, however, is that the obstacle absorbs some of the wave's energy only if half the wavelength is shorter than the obstacle's size.

When physicists work with electromagnetic energy, they use an appropriate mathematical description. When dealing with how electromagnetic energy affects living tissue, they use wave mechanics—what we have been discussing.

Let's put it together. Cells essentially have a fixed size. If half the wavelength of arriving electromagnetic energy is about the size of a cell, then some of the energy will be absorbed by the cell. So if the frequency is high enough, that is if the wavelength is short enough, the cell will absorb some of the energy. The shorter the wavelength, the more energy will be absorbed. Put a pot of water on the stove and add heat. Sooner or later the water will boil. Subject a living cell to electromagnetic energy of an appropriate frequency, and sooner or later it's going to cook. But if the wavelength is long enough, or put another way, if the frequency is low enough, then it really doesn't matter how much energy passes the cell, it won't feel it.

Up until now we have been comfortable with the mathematical analogy of a wave in a pond to help us understand the nature of radiation. Radiation as we are using the word, however, also includes alpha and beta particles, neutrons, and protons. These are not electromagnetic energy. They are physical particles with size and mass. While it is true that in some esoteric quantum mechanical applications, it is still useful to use the wave-in-a-pond analogy when discussing particles, we are not going there.

Time to shift from the pond to the pool table.

The Pool Table

Before we rack the balls, however, let's take a closer look at the high-energy electron. Early atomic scientists named this type of radiation "beta particles" before they determined that it was only high-energy electrons. The name stuck. As subatomic particles go, the electron has relatively low mass, but it carries a full negative electric charge. Remember the little black and white Scottie terrier magnets from your childhood? When placed nose to nose, they repelled each other. Let's conduct a mind experiment. Imagine a pool table with balls that consist of only the noses of these Scottie terrier magnets. Now place them around the table in any configuration you wish. Once you have this picture firmly in mind, imagine rolling one of these "terrier nose" balls across the table. As it moves through your arrangement, other "terrier nose" balls are repelled in all directions, and these repelled balls further repel other balls. By the time your ball reaches the far side of the table, you will have disrupted most of the balls you originally placed on the table.

This is exactly what happens when a beta particle—a high-energy electron—speeds through matter. It disrupts every electron it passes near, and these in turn disrupt others. An atom containing too few or too many electrons is called an ion, and the process of creating ions is called ionization. A beta particle leaves an ionized trail of damage in its wake.

A helium atom stripped of its electrons is capable of causing significant ionizing damage. Early atomic scientists called this an "alpha particle" before realizing what it actually was—they still use the name. Because an alpha particle has a positive electric charge twice as large as the negative electric charge of an electron, for a given distance of travel it can actually cause significantly more ionizing damage. Fortunately, alpha particles typically have very low energy levels. Almost anything will stop them—skin, a piece of paper, a half-inch of air—almost anything at all. Beta particles are a bit more energetic. They can actually penetrate a centimeter of skin and tissue.

A particular hazard exists when a substance that emits either alpha or beta particles is ingested. In this case, the ionizing damage happens directly in possibly vital organs. Another hazard is created when we try to stop beta particles by using a dense material, such as lead. In the process of slowing down, the beta particles interact with the dense nuclei of the damping material, creating X-rays.

Now we need to step back to high-level electromagnetic energy—gamma-rays and X-rays—which I will refer to collectively as high-energy photons. It turns out that these can cause damage in a more subtle way than we have so far examined. A high-energy photon causes damage when it is absorbed, as we discussed earlier. This happens when it directly strikes an electron or even the nucleus of an atom. When this happens the photon can be completely absorbed or deflected like a billiard ball. When it is absorbed into an atom, the atom may give off one or more secondary particles, most of which can cause ionizing damage. When it is deflected, the deflecting atom still will give off one or more ionizing particles. In some cases, another less energetic photon is also given off, which can start the process all over again.

Now rack the billiard balls on the pool table.

Neutrons carry energy as radiation much like electrons, except that neutrons are much heavier, and so can cause more direct damage for a given speed. Imagine the cue ball on a pool table smashing into the array of racked billiard balls. They scatter everywhere, and whatever structure they once had is lost. Since neutrons have no electric charge, they cannot be deflected by a magnetic field like electrons. But the particles released when a neutron collides with an atom often carry significant energy and leave ionized trails of destruction behind them. So neutrons do double-duty damage, directly like a billiard ball and indirectly like the "terrier nose" balls discussed earlier. As with a cue ball striking the racked array of billiard balls, a neutron loses energy with each collision. If it strikes something particularly heavy, like the edge of the table, it retains most of its energy on the rebound. So the way to slow down energetic neutrons is to surround them with much lighter molecules—water, for example. The neutrons give up their energy to the water and slow down, while the water heats up.

Protons carry energy as radiation much like neutrons, and like neutrons, protons are much heavier than electrons and so can cause more direct damage for a given speed. Protons also carry a positive electric charge, so they can be deflected by a magnetic field like electrons. Protons, too, generate double-duty damage.

There is a host of other radiation types—because there is a host of particles with and without mass that can carry energy away from an atom. From an everyday perspective, however, they are relatively unimportant.

A typical cell measures about fifty microns (one millionth of a meter or one thousandth of a millimeter). Generally speaking, any radiation above the level of mid infrared has the potential to affect a cell. There are other factors, of course. How much energy does it take before something actually begins to happen inside a cell? Depending on the nature of the cell, and upon its ability to withstand external forces, it is possible that electromagnetic energy well into the X-ray range will be needed to have a negative effect on individual cells.

We deal with "radiation" every single moment of our lives. It is vital to our existence. Without the sun and its spectrum of radiation, life could not exist. Without the radiative warmth we get from our stoves and furnaces, we would freeze to death. Without the radiation we call radio and television, our lives would be dull and uninteresting.

When radiation is very energetic, however, we must be careful. Sunburn and cataracts are caused by ultraviolet radiation. A hot stove (infrared radiation) can burn. X-rays disrupt cell functions, as can high-energy electrons and neutrons. Alpha and beta particles can be emitted by certain radioactive materials. Alpha particles are not intrinsically dangerous since they cannot penetrate our skin to cause ionizing damage. Beta particles are easily stopped, but they can damage eyes and burn the skin. If ingested, however, so that they come into intimate contact with vital organs, then both alpha and beta particles are extremely dangerous.

By virtue of living on the Earth's surface, we are exposed to ionizing radiation. Literally everything emits some small amount of radiation. In most cases, these levels are so low that they can only be measured with the most sensitive scientific instruments. There are some exceptions, however. Cosmic rays, typically gamma-rays, strike the Earth from every point in space. They originate in the centers of stars, including our own sun. Most cosmic rays are absorbed in the upper atmosphere, but some actually reach the Earth's surface, and some of these strike us. Furthermore, the cosmic rays absorbed by the upper atmosphere create secondary radiation that can strike us on the surface. Our sun produces a prodigious amount of charged particles, which stream past the Earth. Some of these get captured in the Earth's magnetic field and are responsible for the northern and southern lights. Some of these reach the surface to increase our daily radiation dose. Some plants have the ability to concentrate radioactive substances, so that trees, for example, give off more radiation than the ground they grow on.

All Things Radioactive

The Chicken Littles have so dominated today's media that the very word "radiation" strikes fear into the heart of the ordinary person. Yet, as related earlier, we are inundated by radiation every moment of our existence. Have you ever heard that you can get cancer from using a cell phone? Have you heard that living near power transmission lines will make you sick?

Relax on both counts. Cell phone radiation is in the 100-micron region, which is too long to affect your brain, and it has such a low energy level that, even if it could affect your brain cells, there isn't sufficient power to damage them. High-power transmission lines produce much larger energy levels, but their wavelength is about 2,500 miles in air, so you and your house are entirely invisible to the resulting radiation. Consequently, there is no possible danger from either source.

We have already examined the nature of radiation—what it is and what it isn't. By now, we have an understanding of the different kinds of radiation, and even a sense of what radioactivity is. Very few people understand, however, that not only are we inundated by radiation, we are virtually surrounded by radioactivity as well.

Radioactivity is expressed in Becquerels (Bq). One Becquerel is equivalent to one atomic disintegration per second—the release of one alpha or beta particle, or one neutron, or one gamma-ray every second.

Here are examples of the radioactivity level of some common items.

```
1 kg coffee ......................... 1,000 Bq
1 kg granite ........................ 1,000 Bq
1 kg coal ash ....................... 2,000 Bq
1 kg superphosphate fertilizer ........ 5,000 Bq
1 adult human ...................... 7,000 Bq
Air in a typical newer American
    home (radon) ................... 30,000 Bq
1 household smoke detector .......... 30,000 Bq
1 luminous Exit sign ............. 1 trillion Bq
```

This means, for example, that the person standing next to you in the grocery checkout line is experiencing 7,000 atomic disintegrations every second. When you walk into any newer home, you immediately begin to experience 30,000 atomic disintegrations every second due to the radon content of the air. When you walk under the luminous Exit sign at your office, you get hit with the effects of a trillion atomic disintegrations per second.

We continuously experience a relatively constant level of background radiation. In the United States, radiation dosage is measured in rems, or more typically in millirems (one thousandth of a rem). A rem is a unit of ionizing radiation that produces the same damage to humans as one roentgen of high-voltage X-rays—the amount of X-rays that will produce one electrostatic charge of ionization. The typical annual background radiation dose for a human is 360 millirems, or about a third of a rem.

Small amounts of radiation damage are easily repaired by the body. Even small dosages over an extended period have no long-term effect. Similarly, a larger dose taken all at once may cause temporary sickness, although its long-term effect is negligible. Taking a larger dose repeatedly over a short period can, of course, have serious consequences. Taking a really large dose can be deadly, since so much tissue is damaged that the body cannot repair it.

The National Institutes of Health (NIH) has published guidelines for acceptable radiation dosages. NIH sets the annual dosage for the general population at 100 millirems above the naturally occurring background radiation, or just under 500 millirems. On the other hand, for occupational workers, the limit is 5,000 millirems. This is a huge difference, and a case can be made that if it is okay for an occupational worker to experience 5,000 millirems in a year, there is no real reason the general population could not be perfectly healthy with the same annual dosage. In the real world, however, even occupational workers in the nuclear industry never experience such high dosages.

During my twenty-two submerged months aboard nuclear submarines, I wore a radiation badge to measure the total amount of radiation I received. I was within 200 feet of a nuclear reactor the entire time, and as a kicker, because I was the missile officer, I spent a significant part of my time very close to 160 thermonuclear warheads. My total radiation count was actually lower than yours for the same time, no matter where you were. I received essentially no radiation from the reactor and the warheads. The ocean and the submarine hull shielded me from the sun and from cosmic radiation, which pose a millionfold greater risk to humans than do nuclear reactors. The possibility of anybody anywhere receiving a harmful radiation dosage from a nuclear reactor is negligible. We have more important things to worry about, like crossing a busy street.

The Chicken Littles who promulgate their entirely unreasonable and completely incorrect view of radiation and radioactivity, who run about waving their fearful hands in the air, protesting nuclear power plants because they are "dangerous," are—in a word—wrong.

The bottom line is that "radiation" is not a bad word, and it certainly is not something we should fear. Gasoline is very "dangerous" when improperly used. It can explode; it can burn rapidly; it can cause horrific damage under certain conditions. Despite these negative potential problems, we use gasoline every day. All of us, including the Chicken Littles, ride around on a tank of this explosive substance and think nothing of it. We routinely refill our rolling containers without serious thought to the potential danger. We pipe natural gas to millions of homes across the country without serious thought to the fires and explosions that could result from improper usage of this substance. We routinely handle propane and butane, which have similar potential hazards. We store strong acids and alkalis in our homes without a second thought.

We are willing to accept slight risk in exchange for great benefit. This should also be true for radiation. Most radiation is benign as we normally experience it.

Of the radiation that is potentially dangerous, only a small fraction is associated with the generation of atomic power. The risk from this radiation is negligibly small.

This remains true whether or not Greenpeace or Chicken Little agree, or even understand the problem.

CHAPTER 4

Nuclear Power, Solar Power, and Things Beyond

Electricity, in its simplest sense, is electrons flowing through a conductor. We're not talking here about high-energy beta particles but about simple electrons moving relatively slowly in lockstep through an elongated piece of metal. We can pass this flow through a tungsten filament under the right conditions, and we get a glowing light bulb. We can pass it through a special rod consisting of several materials, and the rod gets hot—convenient for space heaters and hot water heaters, among other things. By applying a bit of ingenuity, we can create pulsating rotating magnetic fields that will turn a magnet-covered shaft. We call this a motor.

By reversing this process, by rotating a magnet-covered shaft inside a coil of wire, we can induce an electric current in the wire. In the real world, we frequently use engines or gas turbines to rotate the magnet-covered shaft to produce electricity. At hydroelectric projects across the country, we use water to rotate the shafts. Sometimes we use wind. But very frequently we burn biomass to generate heat to create steam to drive turbines to produce electricity. Of these methods, only hydroelectric- and wind-generated electricity produce no greenhouse gases. While we have determined that the need to reduce greenhouse gases is not a dire emergency, it seems prudent to take reasonable steps over time to lower the amount of these gases we put into the atmosphere. If we could generate the electricity we need safely and efficiently without adding greenhouse gases to the atmosphere, we should examine such an option very closely.

Nuclear Fission

Uranium exists in nature, usually as a pitchblende ore. Pitchblende is mildly radioactive from its load of uranium, which means that it spontaneously emits alpha particles. The level of radioactivity is very low, however, so there is no threat from mining and transporting the ore, and in any case, as we learned earlier, alpha particles pose no threat outside the body anyway. The uranium normally extracted from pitchblende typically takes two different forms, called isotopes: Uranium-235 and Uranium-238. The technical difference between them is that Uranium-238 has three extra neutrons in its nucleus than does Uranium-235. About 99.3 percent of uranium in the Earth's crust is Uranium-238; only about 0.7 percent is Uranium-235, along with a trace percentage of four other isotopes. This is important because the 235 isotope of uranium is the basis of most current nuclear power generation.

Uranium-235 is fissile, which means that it can fission thermally. This means that the nucleus can absorb a thermal neutron and then fission naturally into two pieces plus two or three neutrons plus energy. And a thermal neutron—well, that's a slow or low-energy neutron that has the same temperature as its surroundings; it is said to be in thermal equilibrium. The resulting pieces typically are various isotopes of barium, krypton, strontium, cesium, iodine, and xenon. Both the barium and krypton isotopes subsequently decay by emitting beta particles to form more stable isotopes of neodymium and yttrium. These beta decays, with some associated gamma-rays, make the fission products highly radioactive.

The two or three neutrons created by the fission are, themselves, captured to make the process happen all over again, and again, and again. . . . About 85 percent of the energy released in a nuclear reactor is carried in the motion of these byproducts. About 7 percent is generated by the radioactive decay of the byproducts.

Uranium-238 is not fissile; however, it can capture a thermal neutron, becoming Uranium-239. Almost immediately, it emits a beta particle, becoming Neptunium-239, which also immediately emits another beta particle. This results in Plutonium-239, which is relatively stable and is fissile. Plutonium-239 behaves in much the same way as Uranium-235, producing about one-third of the total energy in a nuclear reactor. Some of the Plutonium-239 captures a neutron to become less stable Plutonium-240, which captures another neutron to become Plutonium-241. This emits a beta particle to become Americium-241, which forms the heart of the modern household smoke detector.

So when you fuel a nuclear reactor with a mix of Uranium-235 and Uranium-238, you get a lot of energy in the form of heat, and some radioactivity as beta particles and gamma-rays. In current American reactors, the final products are a mixture of the elements listed earlier, plus isotopes of plutonium, neptunium, and americium. The latter three emit alpha particles for thousands of years.

Breeder Reactors

In our earlier discussion about how fissile Uranium-235 drives a reactor, we also learned that Uranium-238 participates in the process by transforming into Plutonium-239 which is fissile like Uranium-235. In fact, this isotope of plutonium produces significantly more energy than Uranium-235. And the process continues to produce Plutonium-240 and 241. This raises an interesting question.

Can we take these fuel rods that contain all this plutonium, separate out the plutonium and whatever uranium was not used, and make more fuel rods? You bet. In fact, we actually end up with more fuel after the process than what we started with.

So do we do this? No—at least not in the United States.

So why not, since it seems like a pretty good way to get more fuel?

The answer is pretty dumb. A substantial part of the new fuel is plutonium, as a mixture of the four isotopes 239, 240, 241, and 242. But collectively it is plutonium. Plutonium is used in atomic bombs. The fact that pure Plutonium-239 is what makes an atomic bomb work apparently doesn't matter, because in 1977 President Carter signed a policy that banned the reprocessing of nuclear fuel in the United States. The explanation was that the plutonium could possibly be stolen, and terrorists might be able to use it to make atomic bombs. Never mind that in the real world, it is virtually impossible to separate out the Plutonium-239 from the other isotopes in sufficient purity to use it for bomb making. The process involves using high-precision centrifuges to separate out the various isotopes by weight. The Brits tried it; the Russians tried it; the French tried it; we tried it; but nobody did it very efficiently, even though we had the best scientists and all the money in the world to throw at it. This is why we use an entirely different method for generating the plutonium we use in our nuclear weapons. And if you try to make a bomb with a mixture of plutonium isotopes—forget about it; it won't work, ever. We're talking about the laws of physics here again, folks.

Chicken Little and Greenpeace notwithstanding, unless you have pure Plutonium-239, your bomb will fizzle. So throwing away all that valuable nuclear fuel to prevent terrorists from making a bomb that they can't make anyway is just plain dumb.

So how do we get the Plutonium-239 for our atomic bombs? We built reactors fueled with Uranium-238, whose only job is to create Plutonium-239. These systems are some of the best-guarded plants in the world. Our weapons-grade plutonium is safe. And we use the stuff over and over and over, as necessary, to keep our supply of weapons-grade plutonium up to date and available.

So can we do the same thing to produce nuclear fuel?

The answer is a resounding yes!

This type of reactor, called a Breeder Reactor, actually produces more fuel than it consumes. A reactor designed to use a mixed plutonium fuel is basically the same as the uranium reactor we have already discussed. However, the neutrons that sustain the reaction contain more energy—they are fast neutrons. In order to regulate the internal neutron flux, the primary coolant typically used is one of the light metals, like sodium. Since Uranium-238 is one of the more abundant elements in the Earth's crust, Breeder Reactors make it possible to have an essentially unlimited source of fuel for nuclear reactors—which means an unlimited supply of electricity.

If I don't have your undivided attention yet, try this on for size. At its best, the Breeder system produces no nuclear waste whatsoever; literally everything eventually gets used. In the real world, there actually may be some residual material that could be considered waste, but its half-life—the period of time it takes for half the substance to change into something else—is on the order of thirty to forty years. By contrast, the half-life for the stuff we currently consider nuclear waste is over twenty-five thousand years!

Imagine, no nuclear waste problem. No power shortages. Inexpensive, safe electricity that never runs low. France has constructed and used Breeder Reactors like this for many years. The British use Breeders; so do the Japanese. We invented the technology. It was in our grasp . . . so what happened?

I hesitate to bring up acorns again, but you get the idea.

Nuclear Waste

Okay . . . we made a political decision back in 1977 that has resulted in piles of long-lived radioactive material that we are not supposed to use for anything. Since the half-life for some of this stuff is around 25,000 years, what we do with it is not trivial. Consider that 25,000 years ago, humankind was barely more sophisticated than modern tribes of great apes. And now we have stuff we need to store for another 25,000 years. If you thought the ozone hole was a political football, check this one out.

The first thing we need is a "there" that will be there for the next twenty-five millennia. This is another not-so-trivial decision. Then what we put there needs to stay there, undisturbed for the same twenty-five millennia. Will our descendents 25,000 years from now even be able to read a sign that says Keep Out? Furthermore, do you want this stuff in your backyard?

Neither does anyone else.

The science guys, not the ones who made this stupid decision but the ones who have to carry it out, have solved part of the problem. Researchers have developed a borated glass that appears able to withstand at least ten thousand years of abrasion with little erosion. For now, they encase the nuclear "waste" in borated-glass beads, embed these beads in hardened concrete inside steel drums, and store them in pools of water.

The United States has several thousand such drums just waiting for the politicians to decide into which hole in the ground they will eventually be moved. Store them in old salt mines? Store them in new granite excavations? Store them in an open field surrounded by a fence with signs that read Danger—Keep Out? Sure, why not? It does not matter where you store the encapsulated waste so long as you control access. Radiation given off by encapsulated waste cannot contaminate ground water or the air or anything else. It is akin to radiation from the sun, the open sky, anthracite coal, ancient redwoods—similar, just more concentrated.

It is tempting to believe that our society will progress sufficiently so that one day it will finally decide to make use of this valuable resource. Unfortunately, our guys did a pretty good job with the borated glass. It may turn out to be cheaper to create new nuclear fuel than to undo what we have done.

The final irony is that there is a much better way to dispose of this stuff if we really don't want to keep it around. We tend to think of the Earth as solid. Anybody from San Francisco or Los Angeles can tell you, however, that it ain't so. Our planet's crust consists of a multitude of individual large pieces called tectonic plates. These plates are constantly moving around the surface of the planet, jostling and rubbing one another and sliding over and under each other. When the plate upon which the Indian subcontinent rests bumped into the Asian plate, the resultant crumpling formed the Himalayan mountain chain. When the Eastern Pacific plate hung up while sliding past the North American plate and then let go, the Oakland viaduct collapsed. The Western Pacific plate slides under the Asian plate, forming the Mariana Trench, the deepest spot in the ocean. These forces are enormous, surpassing by orders of magnitude anything else on this planet.

As one plate slides under another, the entire plate edge is forced deep into the bowels of the Earth, where it and everything on and in it is totally transformed into the stuff that makes up the Earth's mantle. This transformation results from tremendous pressure and from heat, caused in part by the pressure and by radioactive substances contained within the Earth.

The Challenger Deep in the Mariana Trench is nearly thirty-six thousand feet deep. This is almost seven miles of water. If you were to truncate Mount Everest at sea level and drop it into the Challenger Deep, there would still be over a mile of water covering the mountain.

If we were to drop the thousands of drums of so-called nuclear waste into the Challenger Deep or some other fast-moving subduction zone, within a few hundreds or thousands of years the material would be pulled deep within the Earth's interior, where it would be utterly dissipated and destroyed. It would become an insignificant part of the radioactivity that already exists within the Earth's mantle, totally indistinguishable from all the rest of the stuff down there.

We have a staggering problem created by a political decision, but we haven't reversed that decision—at least not yet. We could live with it by making another political decision, but we haven't and probably won't.

Long live Chicken Little!

Nuclear Fusion

Nuclear waste is a trivial technical problem but a huge political one. Burning biomass to produce energy is the most popular alternative, but this also produces the highest level of greenhouse gases. One elegant solution solves the entire problem. Simply by switching to Breeder Reactor technology, in one fell swoop we have sufficient power for all our needs into the foreseeable future, we eliminate greenhouse gases as a byproduct of power generation, we eliminate nuclear waste, we eliminate the need to scour the Earth in search of more nuclear fuel, and since a Plutonium mix can't be used for bomb production under any circumstances, this never was a problem in the first place.

Okay, but a Breeder Reactor still is nuclear, and no matter what we say here, the Greens have so poisoned the public mind that we have to win a tremendous uphill battle to enable this solution. As a society, we definitely believe the sky is falling.

Fortunately, a second elegant solution exists, or at least is on the horizon. Fission, as we have learned here, consists of splitting a heavy atom into smaller parts, releasing energy in the process. Some of the original matter actually converts to energy according to Einstein's famous equation: $e = mc^2$. Another nuclear process, called fusion, consists of joining together two light atoms to form a heavier atom, releasing energy in the process—much more energy than with a fission reaction. We observe this reaction in our sun, and we have learned to apply it in a thermonuclear bomb, which is thousands of times more powerful than a nuclear bomb. We haven't quite yet learned, however, to control the fusion reaction as we control fission.

Containing the energy released in a fission reaction is relatively trivial and easily accomplished. We do this literally everywhere on Earth in nuclear reactors. The amount of energy released in a thermonuclear reaction, however, is enormously greater and very much more difficult to contain. Furthermore, the amount of power required to initiate the reaction is very great.

Scientists have been working on the problem since the 1950s, inching towards a solution, but they are not there yet. Several research teams have developed sustained fusion reactions that produce more energy than they use, but the difference is small and the duration is short. Informed scientists insist that it will happen—they just don't know when. So for now, on this one, we watch and wait.

A third elegant answer to the entire problem waits in the wings.

Solar Power

We concluded in the previous chapter that, with a few minor exceptions, all energy on the Earth is either solar power or nuclear power. Obviously, the latter comes from within the Earth. It is energy already present on or in our planet. All we do is release it. Solar energy, on the other hand, originates with the sun, away from our planet. The sun streams energy in all directions. A very small portion of this energy is intercepted by the Earth. By now it should be pretty clear that our planet has struck an energy balance. That is to say that whatever energy from the sun our planet intercepts, it subsequently reradiates back into space. If this were not so, temperatures on the Earth would rapidly rise to intolerable levels. This is, in fact, another way of characterizing the greenhouse effect. If atmospheric conditions on the Earth cause the Earth to retain more energy that it radiates, it's going to get warmer, maybe a lot warmer. And to complete the picture, when this "a lot warmer" eventually generates sufficient cloud cover, the energy equation will: (1) rebalance itself so that the temperature remains relatively constant; or (2) remain unbalanced to the hot side so that things keep getting hotter—which takes us back to the beginning of the argument; or (3) will go the other way, so that it gets colder—maybe a little, perhaps a great deal. Take your pick—nobody knows for sure.

Water consists of hydrogen and oxygen bound together chemically. We have learned that burning plant material—biomass—produces carbon dioxide. The carbon in the biomass combines with the oxygen in the atmosphere to produce carbon dioxide. Burning hydrogen produces only water. Hydrogen combines with the oxygen in the atmosphere to produce water. Herein lies a far-ranging solution to our dilemma.

Capture incoming solar energy, and use it to separate hydrogen and oxygen from water. The resulting hydrogen can then be distributed everywhere through our extensive pipeline network. Hydrogen can be burned like natural gas wherever flame is needed, leaving water as the only byproduct. Hydrogen can drive turbines to generate electricity, leaving water as the only byproduct. Hydrogen can produce electricity directly in fuel cells, leaving water as the only byproduct. Hydrogen can produce heat in space heaters and furnaces without flame, leaving water as the only byproduct. And, of course, hydrogen can be used in the production of many useful chemicals.

It is actually more efficient—translate this as less expensive—to transport energy by pumping hydrogen through pipelines than to transmit energy as electricity over high-tension lines. The way to make this work, then, is to capture solar energy as efficiently as possible and convert it to hydrogen for pipeline distribution.

The most efficient way to capture solar energy is outside the Earth's atmosphere, in orbit. There is a remarkably large number of ways to do this. They range from huge mirrors that concentrate the sun's rays, to sophisticated panels designed to convert sunlight directly into electricity, all the way to the low-tech capture of the sun's heat by water-filled tubes, subsequently using the generated steam to drive turbines to create electricity. The mirrors could beam the energy directly to the Earth's surface, to be captured there for subsequent use to generate hydrogen. The electricity generated by the other methods could be beamed to the surface as concentrated microwaves or even as concentrated laser beams. In the final analysis, however, the energy arrives at the Earth's surface in concentrated useable form.

Our third elegant solution, therefore, is a network of solar-power satellites that beam their collected energy to equatorial marine stations for conversion to hydrogen. We can leave the specifics to the engineers who design the system. The hydrogen is liquefied and transported by ship to shore-based pipeline heads. From there, the hydrogen is distributed nationwide, wherever it is needed. The resultant energy is practically pollution free and makes zero contribution to the global greenhouse.

The Other Options

Are there any other realistic, viable ways to produce power?

Let's examine two that are frequently advocated by nuclear power opponents: locally produced solar energy and ethanol.

Locally produced solar energy, according to energy experts, could realistically supply 50 percent of current domestic hot-water needs. Typically, these generators are panels atop roofs in sunny regions of the country. Generally, they are hot-water panels, but occasionally they are arrays of light-to-electricity generators. In the United States, homes consume about 25 percent of all energy produced. Hot-water production in homes uses about one-third of that. It follows, therefore, that if everyone used solar energy so that 50 percent of our hot-water needs were being met, we would save a scant 4 percent of our national energy needs. It would take an unprecedented national research effort to increase the benefits of locally produced solar energy. Over time more homes will apply these methods. But Chicken Little notwithstanding, moving much beyond the 4 percent level—although better than nothing— seems unlikely.

Ethanol is often touted as a practical solution to our transportation energy needs. Let's examine the economics of this proposal. The current price for corn is about $2.40 per bushel. If we apply available technology optimized for energy and cost savings, we can build a 50-million-gallon-per-year ethanol plant that will convert corn into ethanol for about $1.12 a gallon. This distillation requires large quantities of heat, which we can generate by burning fossil fuel (this seems a bit silly, even though the resulting ethanol is a more concentrated form of energy) or from some other source. One solution is to replace corn as a feed-stock with waste products such as garbage, and to use waste heat from smelters and power generation. Another source for heat is geothermal energy where it is available, or even locally produced solar energy. For the process to be practical, however, the net energy gain must be sufficiently large to offset the cost of the feedstock and the required energy.

If we were to use all the waste generated by food processing, put all existing grain land into productive crop use, and use all surplus sugar and 50 percent of all fermentable municipal solid waste, we could generate 4.7 billion gallons of ethanol in the U.S. each year. This is less than 4 percent of annual U.S. gasoline consumption and less than 2 percent of annual U.S. energy consumption.

The bottom line, then: today in America, if locally produced solar energy were universally applied in its most economically viable form, and if every available means were used to produce ethanol, even discounting the energy required to generate these results, there would be at most a 6 percent annual energy savings.

There is nothing wrong with applying solar energy in economically effective ways. There are great arguments for replacing fossil fuels with ethanol in order to conserve the irreplaceable chemical resources that go up in smoke and heat when we burn them. But a maximum energy savings of 6 percent simply doesn't wash as an argument for abandoning the nuclear energy option.

Electric Cars—Dream or Reality?

Why have pollution-free electric cars never caught on?

Of the many reasons, the most pertinent is the relatively short range of every "practical" electric car developed thus far. Electric cars run on stored electricity. Most research has centered on more efficient batteries. Unfortunately, despite the efforts of a large number of fine scientists and engineers, battery development has been slow, with disappointing results.

When all is said and done, the most practical battery still is a bank of lead-acid cells—basically a bunch of car batteries. Lead-acid batteries are expensive and heavy. It takes twenty or more to keep an electric car running for about a hundred miles.

This might work for commuting, but you had better stay near an electric outlet! As a result, electric cars have never caught on—they're just not practical in today's hectic world.

The hybrid car, which uses a gasoline engine combined

with one or more electric motors, is a stopgap solution. It consumes gasoline to make electricity that runs the electric motors that drive the car. Engineers have developed esoteric ways to recover energy lost when the car slows down, which extends the car's range to make these cars practical for normal driving. Remember, however, that they still burn fossil fuels, producing greenhouse gases, although the exhaust contains less of the other polluting gases than does the exhaust from a traditional internal-combustion engine. Furthermore, these cars cost about one-third more than conventional cars. Nevertheless, they are making inroads in the more densely populated parts of the country.

Then along came Roger Billings, eclectic, entrepreneurial gadfly—and hydrogen researcher.

I first met Roger in 1980 at the Third World Hydrogen Conference in Tokyo. I was there presenting a paper on solar-power satellite production of hydrogen. Roger's presentation followed mine. He had developed a working model of a hydrogen-powered internal-combustion engine. He was not the first to do this, but he had developed one that functioned beyond the limits that researchers in this field thought were absolute. When a staid British professor (the grand old man of hydrogen-fueled internal-combustion engines) interrupted Roger's presentation to inform him that his results were impossible, Roger offered to fly the professor by first class to his lab to inspect a working model.

Billings doesn't believe in limits—which is why he has pushed the limiting envelope again.

A fuel cell is an electricity-generating device. Stored hydrogen is fed into it under proper controls. Inside the cell, hydrogen combines with oxygen from the air to form pure water and electricity. It's that simple—no byproducts, no pollution, absolutely nothing but pure water and electricity. NASA has used fuel cells since the early manned space flights, but outside the space community, fuel cells have always been exotic, expensive toys.

Billings has made the fuel cell practical and relatively inexpensive. His demonstration car can travel 300 miles on one fill-up of hydrogen. At current prices, as a function of distance driven and typical gasoline cost, this translates into an equivalent gasoline price of $1.10 a gallon. The only current drawback is that you cannot drive up to the nearest gas station and "fill 'er up" with hydrogen—yet.

One of the remaining problems is a cheap and practical source of abundant hydrogen. Although hydrogen is one of the more abundant elements on the surface of our planet, most of it is tied up in seawater. It takes power, lots of it, to liberate this hydrogen so it can be used elsewhere. The remaining hydrogen is locked up in natural gas for the most part, with some more available from crude oil. Here, once again, it takes lots of power to liberate it.

We have a planet-wide infrastructure dedicated to generating gasoline from crude oil. The capital investment is enormous, and it cannot simply be ignored. Shec Labs in Saskatoon, Canada, has developed and patented a catalytic method of generating hydrogen from natural gas. The process attained commercial capability in late 2004. In the short term, this technology can begin to replace the gasoline-generating infrastructure, so that the invested capital can continue to work and pay dividends to investors while the industry itself shifts to processes that produce materials instead of something to burn.

More exciting for the future, however, is another Shec development. Shec, Solar Hydrogen Energy Corporation, started out in 1996 when Bob Beck developed a process for producing commercial quantities of hydrogen from water using sunlight. The process has now reached the commercial implementation stage, and a pilot project plant is being constructed. This has the potential for making the dream of a practical electric car a reality.

Fly into any major city on a sunny day. The pall of brown smog hanging over the region will amaze you. Step out into any city street and listen—really listen to the noise level. We are buried in a sea of automobile-generated noise and fumes.

The Billings fuel cell backed up by the Shec process offers a realistic, practical solution. The Billings fuel cell overcomes the chief objection to electric cars: short range (notwithstanding the hybrid, which still pollutes). And the Shec process makes it possible. An electric car can accelerate fast, can be quick and responsive, can be everything we have come to appreciate in personal transportation—without the noise, the heat, the pollution, or the consumption of irreplaceable resources.

With the power-source problem virtually solved, researchers should quickly develop ways of extending the range even further. In hybrids we already see practical flywheels and motor-generator devices that recover energy when the car slows down. These and other developments will eventually double the 300-mile range of the true electric car. That will bring the price down to about fifty cents a gallon.

The Shec process offers an even larger benefit that goes far beyond the impact of electric cars, even though this, by itself, would revolutionize life on Earth. Earlier we discussed how to solve the Earth's energy problems by using a combination of solar-energy-collecting satellites in orbit that beam the collected power to equatorial marine locations where it can be used to generate hydrogen from seawater. When I originally presented a landmark scientific paper on this subject to the Third World Hydrogen Energy Conference, however, there was no practical way to use the incoming power to generate hydrogen.

Shec has solved that problem. We are now on the verge of a new paradigm in energy production and consumption. That it will happen ultimately is inevitable.

What we need is that it happen sooner rather than later. That's worth expending some effort to make it happen.

Cold Fusion

We said earlier that we were in a watch and wait status on the subject of nuclear fusion. While we watch and wait, however, there may be something exciting happening behind the scenes. Several years ago there was a great furor over something called "cold fusion." In Salt Lake City in March 1989, Professors Stanley Pons and Martin Fleischmann announced that under room-temperature conditions, they had observed a nuclear reaction in supersaturated metal hydrides (metals with lots of hydrogen or heavy hydrogen dissolved in them). In the resulting furor, their claims eventually were discredited and these researchers moved to France and England respectively, where they continued their work. Cold fusion research was relegated to the science scrap heap, and only a few dogged researchers continued to follow the leads originally discovered by Pons and Fleischmann. For the most part, they found themselves in a jungle of pseudo-science weirdos, perpetual-motion-machine inventors, and non-peer-reviewed publications.

Recently, however, Dr. Michael McKubre, director of the Energy Research Center at Stanford Research International in Menlo Park, California, and an internationally respected scientist, reported that he has two government-backed independent laboratory verifications of the production of excess heat, tritium, certain isotopes of helium, and a very low level of neutrons. Cold fusion, or "nuclear electrolysis" as Dr. McKubre prefers to call it, is no longer junk science. With this new legitimacy will come regular funding, and the possibility that we may have discovered an inexhaustible supply of safe, inexpensive power.

If nuclear electrolysis turns out to be viable, the entire argument for and against nuclear reactors, Breeder Reactors, hydroelectric power plants, biomass-fired plants, and solar power in all its myriad forms will go away. Power will become a nonissue, something we take for granted like the air we breathe, or daylight and darkness. If this happens, of course, the Greens will have a problem. What sky-is-falling issue will they take up next in their quest to exercise maximum control over you and me?

CHAPTER 5

When Nuclear Goes Wrong

Sometime in late 1984 or early 1985, a Soviet deputy chief engineer with political connections met in Moscow with members of a Politburo subcommittee responsible for oversight of the Soviet nuclear power program. Although his name has vanished along with so many others from this era, his story was related to me personally by three nuclear engineers from the Washington State Hanford Nuclear Reservation who had just returned from an on-site investigation of the Chernobyl disaster.

In the Soviet Union, being a good engineer did not necessarily lead to the "good life." You needed a good political connection, and to rise above the crowd of other politically connected guys, you needed to make your mark. Although not nuclear trained, this deputy chief engineer thought he had discovered a way to save mega-rubles for the Soviet nuclear power program, thereby making the subcommittee members look good and enhancing his own status. This could translate into a larger Moscow apartment, head-of-the-line privileges at the department store, and perhaps even an extra ration of meat or vodka.

Certain Soviet nuclear reactors were shut down for maintenance four times a year. This was a time-consuming process that ultimately cost the subcommittee lots of rubles in lost revenue. The deputy chief engineer convinced Moscow to let him run an experiment on one of these live reactors.

Basically, a nuclear reactor is just a sophisticated machine that creates high-pressure steam to run turbines that generate electricity. Under normal operation, a reactor uses a small portion of the electricity it generates to power coolant pumps that circulate the steam that drives the turbines. Because keeping a reactor cool is critical, all reactors have a set of back-up coolant pumps. When you shut down a reactor, you need an alternative way to power the coolant pumps. Typically, as a reactor shuts down, you keep it cool using the backup or emergency coolant pumps, driven by emergency diesel generators.

The deputy chief engineer's idea was to draw power from the spinning turbine of a reactor that had just shut down and use it to run the emergency coolant pumps while the emergency diesel generators were coming on line. If his idea worked, you could refine the concept to eliminate the need for emergency diesel generators, at a savings of several million rubles per reactor. Although this engineer was not nuclear trained and really knew nothing about nuclear reactors, the nontechnical subcommittee members thought his idea had merit. A successful execution of this concept could lead to a Dacha outside Moscow. They granted permission to run the experiment on one of the older reactors located at the nuclear power generating station in Chernobyl, about eighty miles north of Kiev in the old Soviet Union republic of the Ukraine.

In order to understand what happened next, we need to know something about typical nuclear reactor design.

Nuclear Power 101

All a nuclear reactor really does is produce a lot of heat, heat that can be used to create steam to drive a turbine to generate electricity. When you create steam by burning biomass such as wood, coal, or oil (or even garbage), you must be careful not to expose yourself directly to the fire: it burns. Ditto for heat produced by nuclear fuel: hot is hot. In addition to heat, nuclear fuel produces beta particles, gamma-rays, and ultimately alpha particles. As we learned earlier, there is nothing particularly mysterious about these. They consist primarily of high-energy electrons (the same kind that flow through conductors), high-energy photons (light), and helium ions. They're dangerous because they're energetic and can ionize. A handful of lead pellets poses no danger, but stand in front of a loaded shotgun at your own risk!

A typical reactor is fueled by a mixture containing several forms of refined uranium. This mix is formed into small pellets that are loaded into zirconium tubes. These tubes are then bundled into an assembly called a fuel rod. Fuel rods are placed inside the reactor core, where the uranium mix begins to fission, producing increasing numbers of neutrons until the core goes critical—the reaction becomes self-sustaining. In order to control the reaction process so that the number of neutrons produced equals the number absorbed, control rods made of boron or cadmium are distributed among the fuel rods. These control rods can be adjusted so that the amount of rod material inside the reactor exactly controls the level of neutron production—kind of like a burner knob on a gas stove. Pressurized primary coolant filling the core absorbs the energy released by the fissioning fuel and carries this heat to a heat exchanger, where it is transferred to the secondary coolant. The secondary coolant flashes to steam, which is used to drive the turbine. The steam is condensed back to water in the cooling towers that are characteristic of nuclear power plants.

If something goes wrong at any point, the worst that can happen is the reactor shuts itself off, and it then sits there stewing in its own heat. This can damage internal components of the reactor, but that's it. A nuclear reactor really is nothing more than a device to boil water into steam to drive a turbine. As with any boiler, the steam it creates is under a lot of pressure.

Can it explode?

Not like a nuclear bomb—that's impossible. It's not just unlikely; it is utterly impossible. A nuclear bomb is a runaway chain reaction in fissile material that is tightly contained for several microseconds until the internal pressure builds up sufficiently to cause a gigantic explosion. In a nuclear reactor, the fissile material is not tightly contained. If a runaway chain reaction were somehow to happen, the very worst possible result would be the material gets so hot that it melts and flows around inside the reactor, or perhaps melts out the bottom of a badly designed reactor. That's it. Once it starts flowing around on the floor it cannot maintain its criticality: no more fission, no more heat, and it all stops. The China Syndrome—the idea that a runaway nuclear reactor could somehow melt through the Earth's crust and sink right through to China—is a myth. It cannot happen, ever; the physical laws of the universe prevent it.

A reactor is as likely to explode in a non-nuclear way as any other pressurized steam device. If you build it right, it won't happen. But if something you didn't plan for goes wrong and it does explode, you get a bunch of hot steam, pieces of pipe and boiler, and—unfortunately—unwanted high-energy emissions as well as scrap that emits alpha and beta particles. This is why reactors operate inside containment buildings. Containment buildings are reinforced concrete structures specifically designed to remain intact should there be an explosion of the pressurized reactor core. When properly designed, they contain the products of the explosion—hence their name.

The Soviets designed the Chernobyl reactors according

to the RBMK model. This is an acronym for the Russian *reaktor bolshoy moshchnosti kanalniy,* which means "reactor (of) large power (of the) channel (type)." These are fueled with slightly enriched natural uranium and are water cooled, and the control rods and reactor core casing are made of graphite. This reactor model has three significant advantages over other models: (1) it does not need a high-pressure primary coolant; (2) it produces on average 10 percent more power; and (3) it costs a lot less to build, in part because its low-pressure design eliminates the need for an expensive containment building—at least in principle. Unfortunately, it has one significant disadvantage. Upon failure, it will go "supercritical." Like a snowball rolling down a hill, if something goes wrong, it will continue getting worse until the reactor finally melts to a heap of slag and the fissile material is sufficiently separated that it goes sub-critical.

The Soviet designers of the RBMK reactors recognized this potential danger and built five separate fail-safe mechanisms into their design to shut down the reactor in the event any one of several critical failures happened.

So why take this kind of chance? In the old Soviet Union, like everywhere else, it was all about money. In their centrally controlled economy, the lower construction cost and 10 percent additional power production glittered brightly against a backdrop of superior Soviet technology and engineering, even though they had to shut these reactors down four times a year for maintenance. They took a chance, a calculated risk. Sure it was a stupid thing to do, but they did it.

The Grand Experiment

The deputy chief engineer eventually received permission to run his experiment on Reactor Four at the

Chernobyl nuclear power generating station. He ran his first experiment in mid-1985. The record is not entirely clear, but apparently one of the fail-safe mechanisms designed into the reactor kicked in and shut down the reactor when it sensed that the primary coolant pumps were malfunctioning.

Although red-faced with embarrassment, the deputy chief engineer petitioned for, and eventually received, a second chance from the subcommittee, but apparently he was also told about dire consequences should he fail again.

Midmorning on April 25, 1986, the deputy chief engineer gathered the Reactor Four operating engineers and technicians and explained his plan in detail. He told them how the reactor had shut down the previous year and explained that failure was not an option this time around. He then ordered all five safety systems bypassed, and—just to be sure—he also had all the backup electrical systems shut down, including the emergency diesel generators that could have powered the reactor controls in an emergency.

He probably felt safe doing this because he did not intend on running the reactor for more than a few minutes under load. After all, what could possibly happen in a few short minutes? And, not being nuclear trained, he had no idea of what unintended consequences could result from disconnecting these systems. Although we will never know, he may have been thinking that the worst-case scenario would be a complete shutdown of the reactor as would happen if the fuel supply were cut off from a conventional boiler.

As luck would have it, unexpected power demand that afternoon delayed the experiment until late that evening. In order to get the trial under way, the engineers needed to reduce reactor power to minimum, which—when done by the book—is a time-consuming process. Because they were now behind schedule, they reduced the power level more rapidly than this reactor design could handle. This caused a buildup of neutron-absorbing fission byproducts in the reactor core, which poisoned the reaction and threatened to shut it down altogether. Since that would have spoiled the experiment a second time (hello, Siberia), to compensate, they withdrew most of the control rods. Because of the poisoning, this allowed a power increase to barely thirty megawatts, which was just sufficient to bring the reactor into its most unstable range. Something had to be done immediately.

There were only two choices: do absolutely nothing and wait twenty-four hours for the poisoning to dissipate, or increase the power immediately.

With Siberia in the wings, you know what choice they made.

They finally marginally stabilized reactor power at 200 megawatts—one-fifth its design power. In the process, because the reaction was still poisoned, they had pulled all but 6 of the 211 rods. The absolute design minimum for this reactor was 30 rods left in the core, so the immediate situation was dire.

About a half-hour later, as things appeared reasonably stable, they decided to commence the actual experiment, and shut down the turbine generator. Their intent was to see if the turbine could still supply coolant pump power even though it was only coasting—no longer being driven by the reactor. A successful outcome would prove that they did not need to obtain outside power to maintain proper cooling levels when they decoupled a reactor and its turbine. An engineer with nuclear training could have told them the answer without conducting the experiment. But the deputy chief engineer wasn't a Nuke.

With reduced electrical power, the pumps slowed, reducing the flow of cooling water.

The modern nuclear reactor used in the United

States and the rest of the world controls neutron levels by absorbing them with boron or cadmium rods. The primary coolant acts as a moderator by slowing the neutrons. The RBMK model, however, works in reverse, using graphite rods to moderate the neutrons and the primary coolant to absorb them.

So we have a reactor operating at a significant power level with almost all the moderating control rods pulled. It is still stable, although barely, because the primary coolant is absorbing neutrons as fast as they are being produced. Now slow the coolant pumps so the water moves more slowly. It stays in the reactor core longer, getting hotter, and finally begins to boil. But steam cannot absorb neutrons; suddenly the neutron flux skyrockets.

The reactor operators immediately hit the emergency button that drives the control rods, all remaining 205 of them, and the emergency protection rods into the core. But all backup power had been shut down, even the emergency diesel generators. The only available power came from the slowing turbine, which meant that the already slow primary coolant pumps had even less power. So the entire cycle was exacerbated.

This is when another design problem of the RBMK became evident. The control rods had graphite tips followed by a one-meter hollow segment (I don't know why; they just did) followed by a five-meter graphite section. As soon as the rods penetrated the core, they displaced more coolant without themselves absorbing any neutrons, because of the hollow section. The already skyrocketing neutron flux went ballistic. All hell broke loose, and the reactor container exploded—not a nuclear explosion, just a plain, old-fashioned steam-boiler explosion.

But it was a doozy. Red-hot chunks of fuel and graphite fell everywhere. Fifty tons of nuclear fuel evaporated and were ejected high into the atmosphere. Seventy tons were ejected sideways into the surrounding areas. An additional 50 tons of fuel and 800 tons of graphite remained in the reactor vault, smoldering for days. Experts have placed the release of radioactivity at about ten times the amount generated at Hiroshima.

The Chernobyl Aftermath

A plume of radioactive fallout swept across Europe, leaving measurable contamination as far away as Finland. There was a veritable continent-wide panic. Whole towns were evacuated, and strange symptoms popped up in places where the fallout could not have reached, no matter what the circumstances.

In the final analysis, however, the health consequences were relatively small. According to the Nuclear Energy Agency (a specialized agency within the Organization for Economic Co-operation and Development, an intergovernmental organization of industrialized countries, based in Paris), as of April 2001, a total of thirty-one persons had died as a direct consequence of the accident; they were all either plant personnel or directly involved in fighting the fire following the explosion. One hundred forty individuals from these same groups had suffered varying degrees of radiation sickness and health impairment, but all of these individuals recovered fully with no permanent consequences. Between 1990 and 1998, in the regions affected by the explosion and subsequent fallout, 1,791 cases of thyroid cancer were diagnosed and assumed to have been caused by the radiation release.

The deaths and injuries are tragic, of course. But this is a far cry from the misinformation contained in a Greenpeace Web site commemorating the tenth anniversary of the Chernobyl disaster, which stated flatly that 2,500 people were killed, millions were affected, and hundreds of thousands displaced.

This was a stupid, completely unnecessary accident resulting from gross criminal negligence and total managerial incompetence, but it was not caused by a nuclear problem. This problem could only have happened within a political system that was completely out of contact with the real world. There is not the slightest possibility such an accident could ever occur anywhere else, first because the RBMK reactor is not used anywhere else and second because the controls in place everywhere else would absolutely prevent such a situation from developing, even if it could somehow commence.

The entire tragedy hinged upon the reactor becoming unstable when the coolant slowed, but this can only happen in the RBMK reactor, and nobody, absolutely nobody else, uses this model. All other reactors would have shut themselves down, period. The physical laws of the universe make it so, no matter what Greenpeace and the other Chicken Little nuclear fear mongers say.

Three Mile Island

On March 26, 1979, at the Three Mile Island nuclear complex near Middletown, Pennsylvania, reactor operators conducted a test of the emergency feedwater system for the Three Mile Island Unit 2 (TMI-2). This is a routine test to verify that the reactor backup cooling system functions correctly. This backup system is designed to supply emergency cooling of the reactor in the event of failure of the secondary cooling system. In effect, this system supplies a secondary source of water to extract heat from the primary coolant. Part of this routine test requires that a valve accessing emergency secondary coolant be shut at the beginning of the test and reopened at the end of the test. Somebody goofed—made a serious mistake—and this valve was not reopened. This shut valve did not affect normal reactor operation but, when shut, prevented emergency secondary coolant from reaching the heat exchanger in the event of failure of the normal secondary coolant source.

One of the routine safety precautions used in nuclear power plants is to maintain a strict separation between the water used to cool the core directly—the primary coolant—and the water used to drive the turbine—the secondary coolant. Heat collected by the primary coolant is transferred to the secondary coolant in a heat exchanger, which essentially is a boiler wherein the secondary coolant is circulated around metal tubes containing the primary coolant. The two coolants never actually contact each other.

On March 28, 1979, a problem developed in the secondary coolant pumps of TMI-2. At about four o'clock in the morning, a mechanical or possibly electrical failure caused them to stop.

As a result, both the turbine and the reactor automatically shut down, just as they were designed to do. When the secondary pumps failed, the still undiscovered shut valve prevented the emergency feedwater system from taking up the slack. Eight minutes into the incident, someone discovered the shut valve and opened it. Consequently, nuclear reactions were still happening during these eight minutes without any secondary cooling.

The normal consequence of such a shutdown is that pressure inside the reactor increases, because the heat is no longer being removed. A reactor vessel contains a pressure-relief valve that functions similarly to the pressure-relief valve on a household pressure cooker. At TMI-2, this valve opened to decrease internal reactor pressure. Unfortunately, the valve failed in the open position—it was stuck open—and to complicate matters, when it failed, it also broke the transmitter that indicated the valve's position to the operator. Consequently, the operator did not realize that the valve was open. Had he known this, he could have shut it manually. But it remained open, so that the internal reactor pressure continued to drop, as primary coolant flowed out of the core into the pressurizer and out the stuck valve.

TMI-2 provided no way to read the level of coolant in the core directly. Instead, operators read the level from a gauge on the pressurizer, and because the core and pressurizer were connected directly to one another, they deduced the level of coolant in the core. In the meantime, however, underpressure in the primary coolant system caused by the stuck-open pressure-relief valve created steam bubbles throughout the primary coolant system. These bubbles caused the pressurizer to fill with water, giving a false reading that the primary system was filled to capacity. The operator stopped adding water to the primary coolant system, even though such additional water was critically necessary—another big mistake.

The result of all this was that a gas bubble formed at the top of the reactor vessel, and the fuel rods sustained significant heat damage because they were not cooled adequately. Furthermore, some of the gas was released into the containment building, carrying with it nuclear byproducts, contaminating the air in the building. To complicate matters further, some primary coolant carrying radioactive debris from the damaged fuel rods leaked from the system and found its way into the building's basement. There it evaporated and condensed on the walls, adding more nuclear byproducts to the already contaminated interior.

After all was said and done, the actual release of radioactive material into the environment was about the equivalent of eight radioisotope sources for medical diagnosis, or about nine thousand luminous Exit signs. This is not a lot of radioactivity, especially since the material was dispersed into the atmosphere. The average radiation dose received by residents near Three Mile Island was only 1.4 millirems, compared to a typical annual background dose of 360 millirems. This is about the same amount you would receive from cosmic radiation on a flight from New York to Los Angeles.

Clearly the Three Mile Island incident did not endanger anybody. It took the court system ten years to validate this conclusion. The worst nuclear accident in United States history harmed absolutely nothing.

The 1979 Three Mile Island accident was caused by a sequence of errors—mechanical and human. Nevertheless, despite the outcry from the Chicken Little set, everything remained inside the containment building. There was essentially no release of harmful emissions. Had people reacted properly to the initial problem instead of running around screaming that the nuclear sky was falling, the plant could be in production today. More importantly, should a similar sequence of events happen in a nuclear power plant today, the outcome would be a minor local problem, and the plant would be back on line in a few days.

CHAPTER 6

Reading, 'Riting, and 'Rithmetic, Taught to the Tune of . . .

In April 1983, David Pierpont Gardner, president of the University of Utah and president elect of the University of California, signed a letter to the then secretary of education, the Honorable T. H. Bell. The letter was authored by the eighteen members of the National Commission on Excellence in Education, which had been established by Secretary Bell on August 26, 1981. The members of this commission consisted of educators from all levels, presidents of large and small universities, corporate presidents, a Nobel laureate, scientists, a governor, and government officials. The letter introduced the commission report, *A Nation at Risk*.

Quoted directly from their report, the commission charter was to:

- Assess the quality of teaching and learning in our Nation's public and private schools, colleges, and universities;
- Compare American schools and colleges with those of other advanced nations;
- Study the relationship between college admissions requirements and student achievement in high school;
- Identify educational programs which result in notable student success in college;
- Assess the degree to which major social and educational changes in the last quarter century have affected student achievement; and

- Define problems which must be faced and overcome if we are successfully to pursue the course of excellence in education.

The commission concluded that "declines in educational performance are in large part the result of disturbing inadequacies in the way the educational process itself is often conducted."

A Nation at Risk was widely read and discussed. Some of the recommendations were implemented locally, and in some areas nationally. A vigorous "school voucher" movement sprang up across the country. The idea was being put forward that choice and competition work well in commerce, so why should they not work equally well in education. The concept appeared in many guises, sometimes as carefully thought out proposals for completely revamping how we finance our education system and sometimes as thinly disguised diversions of public money into the hands of religious educators.

Not unexpectedly, the power brokers in the education bureaucracy dug in their heels. The National Education Association (NEA), seeing itself at serious risk, came out swinging. The NEA acknowledged in a general way that there was a problem, which it promised to address using its combined expertise and clout (never mind that the commission had indicted the NEA in particular for its role in the problem). Its entrenched leaders identified the school voucher movement as the most immediate threat to their own power base. They enlisted every supporter they could find, calling in all markers.

The NEA used an ingenious two-pronged approach. In the United States there is a pervasive and possibly justified suspicion of a significant part of the private-school establishment. Many of these schools are seen as a thinly disguised way to circumvent the teaching of modern science and in particular modern biology in favor of what is sometimes called creation science. The NEA focused on this uneasiness. In its public announcements, discussions, and commissioned articles, it never referred simply to "school vouchers" but always to "private-school vouchers." Having made this point, the NEA then hauled out the constitutional separation of church and state, loudly proclaiming that private-school vouchers violated our basic ideals.

The NEA's second objection follows directly from its distortion of the phrase "school vouchers" into the phrase "private-school vouchers." The argument goes like this. Removing direct funding of the public schools by giving parents private-school vouchers removes this funding forever from the public-school arena and places it in the hands of private educators. Since poor people cannot afford to attend private schools even with a private-school voucher in hand, their children will be forced to attend now seriously financially strapped public schools. Moreover, the NEA argues, private schools have the ability to reject any student they wish, further eliminating effective schooling for those members of our society who need it most.

This is an old debater's trick. Completely destroy your opponent's position with contrived flaws. This approach seems to have worked. The NEA tirelessly preached this message. It was repeated at every state level as well. Every referendum for some form of school choice was met with fierce opposition generated by the NEA. One can only imagine the degree of lobbying and the sums of money that went into these efforts.

Time passed, and major changes to the education system were not forthcoming. So the NEA backed away from its militancy, and things pretty much got back to normal. Over time, public interest turned to other things, and a general complacency crept into the national psyche. The economy prospered. People prospered. The

World Wide Web prospered. The dot.coms prospered. Times were good.

Things went thus for fifteen years. A generation of children untouched by *A Nation at Risk* completed K through 12. It was time to reassess, to reevaluate how we were doing compared to fifteen years earlier and, more importantly, compared to the world stage.

A Nation Still at Risk

In the spring of 1998, thirty-eight distinguished individuals met at a summit sponsored by the Center for Education Reform, the Hudson Institute, and the Heritage Foundation. Several of these were former members of the National Commission on Excellence in Education. They represented a spectrum of citizens— educators, scholars, scientists, corporations, foundations, and government officials. On April 3, 1998, this distinguished group filed a report titled *A Nation Still at Risk: An Education Manifesto.*

Comparing their findings to those from fifteen years earlier casts a special light on the situation as it was and is and points to several avenues for solving this complex problem. The earlier commission discussed its findings in a general way and then detailed four areas of special interest: content, expectations, time, and teaching. The members of the 1998 summit followed suit.

The 1983 commission determined that when compared with other industrialized nations, on nineteen international academic tests American students were never first or second and were last seven times. As measured by the simplest tests of everyday reading, writing, and comprehension, 23 million American adults were functionally illiterate. Thirteen percent of American seventeen-year-olds were functionally illiterate, and this number jumped to 40 percent for minority youths.

College Board Scholastic Aptitude Tests (SATs) demonstrate a seventeen-year unbroken decline from 1963 to 1980. Math and verbal scores fell forty and fifty points respectively. National assessments of science in 1969, 1973, and 1977 revealed a steady decline in seventeen-year-old achievement scores. Remedial math courses in public four-year colleges increased by 72 percent between 1975 and 1980, and in 1983 they constituted one-quarter of all math courses taught in these institutions.

Business and military leaders complained in 1983 that they had to spend millions of dollars teaching new recruits such basic skills as reading, writing, spelling, and computation. Academic achievement for over half the "gifted" students failed to match their tested ability.

That was 1983. Fifteen years later things had changed.

The Third International Math and Science Study (TIMSS) shows that out of twenty-one industrialized nations, American twelfth graders rank nineteenth in mathematics and sixteenth in science. We're no longer discussing third or fourth place; now we're talking about the bottom of the heap. Adult functional illiteracy has doubled, approaching 50 million. Young-adult illiteracy is approaching 25 percent as measured by the 1994 National Assessment of Educational Progress.

SAT scores actually gained two points on verbal and eleven points on math, but the average combined score in 1995 was still seventy points lower than in 1963, before the infamous recentering made the actual number scores appear similar. The performance of seventeen-year-olds on the science portion of the National Assessment of Educational Progress also increased slightly, but the 1994 average still remained lower than in 1969. In 1995, 30 percent of college freshmen enrolled in at least one remedial course, which 80 percent of all public four-year universities offered.

U.S. manufacturers reported that 40 percent of seventeen-year-olds lack the math skills and 60 percent lack the reading skills to hold down a production job. American physics and advanced math students scored dead last among sixteen nations on the advanced portion of the TIMSS test.

Despite the efforts of the NEA—or maybe because of these efforts—the general education picture is more grim after fifteen years of effort than when the report first appeared.

When addressing content, the 1983 commission reported that secondary-school curricula had been homogenized, diluted, and diffused to the point that they no longer had a central purpose. It described a cafeteria-style curriculum in which appetizers and desserts were mistaken for main courses. From 1964 to 1979, the proportion of students taking "general track" courses of study instead of vocational and college preparatory courses increased from 12 to 42 percent. Twenty-five percent of the credits earned by these students were in physical and health education, work experience outside the school, remedial English and math, and personal service and development courses, such as training for adulthood and marriage. Only 31 percent of high-school graduates completed intermediate algebra; only 16 percent completed geography; and only 13 percent completed basic French. Where it was offered, only 6 percent of students completed calculus. Only 14 percent of high-school graduates had completed a core curricula of four years of English and three each of math, science, and social studies.

Significant improvement was found in 1998. From 1982 to 1994, high-school graduates taking college preparatory courses rose from 9 to 39 percent, while the percentage taking a vocational program dropped from 23 to 6 percent. Intermediate algebra completion rose from 31 to 58 percent; geography completion rose from 16 to 25 percent; basic French completion rose from 13 to 18 percent; and calculus completion rose from 6 to 16 percent. Overall, basic core curricula completion rose from 14 to 39 percent.

When addressing expectations, the 1983 commission reported that the amount of homework for high-school seniors had decreased to less than an hour a night; yet grades rose even as average student achievement declined. It reported that many other industrialized nations begin teaching math, biology, chemistry, physics, and geography as mandatory classes in grade six. Students in these countries spend three times as many class hours on these subjects as even the most science-oriented American students.

Only eight states required high schools to offer foreign-language instruction, but none made it mandatory for students to take it. Thirty-five states required only one year of math, and thirty-six required only one year of science. Thirteen states allowed students to choose 50 percent or more of their graduation units, which resulted in many students selecting less-demanding, personal-service courses, such as bachelor living. Minimum competency examinations were required by thirty-seven states, but they fell short of what was needed, because the "minimum" tended to establish a threshold that became a de facto standard, thus lowering the overall educational standards.

By 1998, the percentage of high-school seniors reporting doing less than one hour of homework a night had not changed. Although thirty-eight states had drafted academic standards in the core subjects of English, math, science, and social studies, and thirty-four states were using standards-based assessments of math and English, there was no move whatsoever to begin teaching math, biology, chemistry, physics, and geography in the years before high school.

The Thomas B. Fordham Foundation studied standards-based assessments. It looked for rigorous, clear standards and found only one state having them in English, one in history, three in geography, three in math, and six in science. It assigned failing grades for their standards to twelve of twenty-eight states in English, nineteen of thirty-eight in history, eighteen of thirty-nine in geography, sixteen of forty-eight in math, and nine of thirty-six in science.

By 1996, four states required students to take a foreign language in order to graduate. Twenty-six states required two or fewer years of math, and thirty-two required two or fewer years of science. By 1994, only 41 percent of high-school courses were mandatory.

Evidence presented to the 1983 commission demonstrated three disturbing facts about the use that American schools and students made of time: (1) compared to other nations, American students spent much less time on schoolwork; (2) classroom and homework time is often used ineffectively; and (3) schools are not doing enough to help students develop either the study skills to use time well or the willingness to spend more time on schoolwork.

In other industrialized countries, the typical school day is eight hours, 220 days a year. In the United States, by contrast, it is only six hours for 180 days. Some schools provided students with only seventeen weekly hours of academic instruction, with the average being about twenty-two. Furthermore, time spent learning how to cook and drive counted as much towards graduation as time spent studying math, English, chemistry, history, or biology. When the commission examined how the classroom time was actually used, it discovered that some California elementary students received only one-fifth of the instruction others received. In most schools, teaching study skills was haphazard and unplanned. Consequently, many students completed high school and entered college without disciplined and systematic study habits.

By 1991, the average American school year had actually declined by two days, and remained a full twenty days shorter than the international average. The 1994 report of the National Commission on Time and Learning estimated that French, German, and Japanese students receive more than twice as much core academic instruction over four years as American students. Seventy-six percent of professors and 63 percent of employers believe that "a high school diploma is no guarantee that the typical student has learned the basics." Most of these professors and employers judge students weak on skills needed to succeed in college or on the job.

The 1983 commission found that not enough of the academically able students were being attracted to teaching; that teacher preparation programs needed substantial improvement; that the professional working life of teachers is unacceptable; and that a serious shortage of teachers exists in key fields.

The commission determined that too many teachers were being drawn from the bottom quarter of graduating high-school and college students. Teacher training was weighted heavily with how-to-teach courses at the expense of courses in subjects to be taught. Forty-one percent of an elementary-school teacher candidate's time is spent in education courses, which reduces the time available for subject-matter courses.

The average teacher's salary in 1983 after twelve years of teaching was only $17,000 per year. Many teachers had to supplement their income with part-time and summer employment. In addition, individual teachers had little influence in such critical professional decisions as, for example, textbook selection. A severe shortage existed for math, science, and foreign-language teachers, as well as specialists in education for gifted and talented, language minority, and handicapped students. In 1981, forty-three of forty-five states revealed math teacher shortages, thirty-three for earth sciences, and all forty-five for physics. Half the newly employed math, science, and English teachers were not qualified to teach these subjects, and fewer than one-third of American high-school physics courses are taught by qualified teachers.

Fifteen years later, fully 40 percent of public high school science teachers and 34 percent of math teachers had neither an undergraduate major nor a minor in their main teaching fields. Fifty-six percent of high-school physical science students, 27 percent of math students, and 21 percent of English students were taught by out-of-field teachers. In public schools populated by a high percentage of low-income students, 47 percent of teachers had neither a college major nor minor in their main assignment fields.

The good news is that by 1992, SAT scores of prospective education majors rose by forty-seven points, but the bad news is that they still trailed the national average by forty-nine points. In 1990, 34 to 36 percent of teachers reported they had control over selecting textbooks, selecting course content and topics, and disciplining students. The average public-school teacher salary in 1996-97 was up 12 percent in real terms from 1983, to $38,509.

Another consequence of business as usual in our education system is that we are developing a dual school system. Moderate to well-to-do neighborhoods have schools that typically fall near the top of the dismal performance curve we have been discussing. These schools are not necessarily good, but they are far ahead of most schools in poor neighborhoods. We have recreated a school system that is separate and unequal. It is already difficult for an educationally handicapped upper-middle-class school graduate to compete in the modern world. How much more difficult it must be for the graduate of a poor-neighborhood school where not one of the student's teachers was qualified to teach math, science, geography, English, or history.

Many disadvantaged students will never overcome the emotional and vocational schism created by this difference in how we deliver even the mediocre product we offer. Our education system is promoting a growing chasm between the haves and the have-nots. Unlike the haves, who can still compete, albeit ineffectively, the have-nots never learn in school how to compete in the first place. Survival is all they learn, survival at the expense of the haves. When you've got nothing, and when you've got nothing to lose, violence is a ready means to take what you don't have.

We the People v. the NEA

One of the fundamental issues that sets the United States apart from all other nations is codified in the Preamble to the Constitution, where the words "We the People" appear prominently as the lead-in, and in the Tenth Amendment: "The powers not delegated to the United States by the Constitution, nor prohibited by it to the States, are reserved to the States respectively, or to the people."

In other words, in our country the individual reigns supreme.

We are a divergent nation with many points of view and many ways of accomplishing a task, but underlying all that is the simple principle that the individual is more important than the group, and the local group is more important than the national group. We are, fundamentally, a bottom-up organization, with all power ultimately deriving from the people. It is very easy to see this principle in play in our business lives. In fact, we exercise this principle so firmly that we frequently attempt to use government power to keep private business from growing so large that it becomes a top-down oppressor.

The Constitution forces our government entities to comply with this principle. We use the law to force business to comply with this principle, although many business have discovered on their own that they become much more profitable by voluntarily developing their own versions of bottom-up management.

One important area of our society has completely escaped this pattern of bottom-up governance. Our K-through-12 education establishment, under the tight-fisted control of the NEA, has developed a top-down hierarchy unrivaled by any other structure in our society, except perhaps the military.

It is especially interesting to review the current NEA guiding philosophy that was first established back in the 1930s. Before then, the NEA was properly concerned with educational issues, but with the publication of the thirteenth annual report of the NEA's Department of Superintendence, the focus shifted to political and economic issues. This report is preoccupied with issues like the merits of central planning and the collective ownership of the means of production. Here are some selected quotes from that report:

- The earlier individualism of the competitive, laissez-faire system simply does not fit the corporate, closely integrated society of the power [read "mechanized"] economy. Until many of these hang-over ideas and ideals are cleared away we shall continue to be crippled in our attempts to create the necessary new social procedures and accompanying institutions [page 121].

- The time has come when our social philosophy must be made to correspond to the world in which we now live. This involves among other things the frank acceptance of the collective economy [page 122].
- Community services such as health, education, . . . travel, and recreation could be indefinitely expanded to the advantage of all. . . . The state is the only agency which can adequately support and administer these services for the community as a whole [page 130].
- New methods of distributing social income will have to be devised. . . . Neither can the device of "free" competition in the open market be exclusively trusted to fix the remuneration of the individual [page 131].
- From the standpoint of magnitude of operations and numbers employed, many of our large privately owned corporations are, in fact, public undertakings. To place these huge enterprises under public ownership, thereby restoring ownership and control of the tools to those who actually work with them, need in no way lessen the amount of private initiative and personal liberty [page 132].
- It is no longer a question of economic planning and control versus free competition and private enterprise under laissez faire. For better or worse laissez faire is dead [page 133].

Is this beginning to sound familiar?

We have an organization with control over our entire pre-college public-school system whose operating manual reads like a page out of Karl Marx or Friedrich Engels. Never mind that the Soviet Union collapsed like a house of cards, due almost entirely to its reliance on centralized control and collective ownership of the means of production. Never mind that the Socialist agenda is one of the most discredited in the world. Is it any wonder that our educational system is in shambles? It is surprising, actually, that it has lasted so long.

The Teaching Experience

Consider this. All the way up to the Kennedy administration, a talented, educated, motivated woman really had only two satisfying career options. She could become a registered nurse or she could become a schoolmarm. Of course, there were exceptions. Nevertheless, each member of our society who attended school before 1960 can recall several of these wonderful, dedicated human beings. These ladies indelibly imprinted thousands of young lives during their careers.

Our society has changed dramatically since then. A career-oriented woman who might have become an influential teacher in the 1930s, 1940s, and 1950s probably is a well-paid doctor, attorney, or executive today. Back then, some of the best female minds in our society were schoolteachers. Today, very few women of this caliber choose to teach—and rightly so. The hours are long, the pay is poor, and job satisfaction almost nonexistent. Free individuals in a free society must be able to choose what is best for them.

While these women still ruled America's classrooms, no matter how poorly the top-down structure mandated by the NEA functioned, children were going to learn to read, write, and calculate, period. Remove the top 20 percent of any group, however, as has happened with America's teacher corps, and you significantly lower its average ability. Combine this with a governing body that still thinks Marx was a misunderstood good guy, ineffective parental supervision, single-parent environments, rampant drug use, and a mindset that apparently emphasizes mediocrity over excellence, and you get young adults who can't compete on the world stage. Is it any wonder that America is falling behind competitively—in quality production, in research, in engineering?

Several years ago, one of my colleagues was attending graduate school in Miami, Florida. His assigned roommate, Jimmy, was a young man working on his master's degree in order to teach junior high school mathematics. My colleague was relatively unimpressed with Jimmy's abilities, but towards the end of his stay he found Jimmy deep into studying for his final examinations. Jimmy explained that he would have to demonstrate expertise in every phase of mathematics before he would be allowed to teach the subject, and he was straining to meet the requirements. Impressed by this, my colleague was prepared to reassess his entire take on the matter. He examined the volume that was giving his roommate such difficulty.

"Jimmy," he said, "this is just ordinary compound fractions."

"Yes," Jimmy answered, "and they are so terribly difficult, aren't they?"

When we start with mediocrity, how can we expect better than mediocre results?

While they were teachers, the top women in the profession kept it together, kept the system from falling apart despite its fatal internal flaws. With their absence, the system has come apart at the seams. The 1983 commission identified many of the specific problems and pointed to what it thought might be answers. So what happened? Why, fifteen years later, was the system significantly worse, with a few small exceptions?

It all comes down to power. The NEA had and has the power to maintain the status quo. Never underestimate the power of the lobbying dollar. The NEA has spent millions of dollars to support specific legislation and to underwrite specific candidates that will ensure its continuing place in the education bureaucracy. The NEA acknowledged the problem identified in 1983 and then made a token effort to solve it, until the public no longer seemed to care. Then it was back to business as usual.

Again, it all comes down to power. Those of us with the means have been able to sidestep many of the problems of the public-school system, either by funneling money and influence directly into a specific local school, or by taking our children out of public education altogether and placing them in schools where children still receive a meaningful education. In effect, these individuals know exactly how to reap benefits from an existing system, how to turn it to their advantage, and how to sidestep it entirely when it no longer serves their purpose.

But what about the millions of poor and minority children whose parents have no power, and may not even be aware of the options available to more affluent members of our society? A typical African-American welfare mother is every bit as interested in seeing her child achieve as her white, suburban, middle-class counterpart. In fact, she may be even more motivated, since she is so near the bottom of the well. Yet her only option is a lackluster school with inadequately trained teachers, the most rigid bureaucracy, and the shoddiest quality.

Market Education

In his 1999 book *Market Education, the Unknown History,* Andrew Coulson examined the history of education from the time of Plato and the Greek Golden Age right up to yesterday's news, ironically something no one else has ever done. He asked a simple question: "What has worked historically, and what has not worked?"

Coulson deduces that "five interrelated traits [have characterized] every consistently successful school system for the last two and a half thousand years: choice and financial responsibility for parents, and freedom, competition, and the profit motive for schools—in essence, a free market in education."

If history has taught us anything, it is that we can learn from history; we don't need to retry all the things that have failed in the past. We can, instead, build on those things that worked in earlier times, adapting them to modern circumstances and using them to our best advantage.

Coulson tells us that throughout the past 2,500 years, effective schools served parents who had a choice in the school, the curriculum, the teachers, and the administration and who were financially involved in the operation of the school. In other words, they had a stake in every aspect of the school, including its source of funding. Recognizing that a free market based school system still must meet the needs of all families regardless of their financial circumstances, he discusses several approaches to the funding problem, including school vouchers and tax credits (which are two sides of the same coin), charter schools, and private management of public schools.

After discussing each of these funding approaches in depth, Coulson concludes that the best approach is a network of private scholarships competing with one another, offering access to the entire spectrum of possible schools. He argues that this solution answers most of the objections raised by opponents to each of the other funding proposals, including direct public funding of public schools as currently practiced. He even develops a plan that will enable an orderly transition from our current system of publicly funded public schools and privately funded private schools to a free market system. This new system would finally enable American children to reach their educational potential, and America to take its rightful place as the nation with the best-educated citizens on the planet.

The answer is not school vouchers, not charter

schools, nor turning over management of our public schools to private firms. And it certainly is not applying Band-Aid fixes to specific problems identified in the 1983 commission report, *A Nation at Risk,* or its follow-up fifteen years later.

The answer is radical, but very American, unlike the Marx- and Engels-driven solutions the NEA keeps trying to impose on a system it bears a large measure of responsibility for ruining. The inescapable conclusion from Coulson's research is that for the last two and a half thousand years, the only school systems demonstrating long-term effectiveness were those offering parents a choice in the school, the curriculum, the teachers, and the administration and requiring their financial involvement in the operation of the school.

It's time we applied this dramatic lesson from history.

Education and Training

As a college student in the 1960s, I attended an upper-level meteorology course. My classmates and I had successfully completed the requisite math courses; nevertheless, we quickly discovered that our marginal Tensor Analysis skills would prevent us from passing the course. Our instructor interrupted the course to teach us the necessary mathematics.

Did we join this class with insufficient education, or with insufficient training? In this class, were we being educated or trained?

Consider my final examination for an upper-level marine physics course. The professor arrived fashionably late, dropped several hundred-page examinations on his desk, and left the room. We had two hours to complete the exam. It turned out this was really not even sufficient time to absorb fully each of the professor's questions.

After a brief discussion among ourselves, we apportioned the questions, which we discovered were quite interrelated, and attacked the final exam as a group problem to which we each would contribute part of the solution. Since we were given no guidelines, and since the test was "open book," there appeared to be no reason we could not do this. As it turned out, this is exactly what the professor hoped we would do. It gave him a very good measure of how we had learned to think through a problem, work together as the real world demands, and make individual contributions to a common solution.

Beyond the training he imparted, this professor taught us to think—he educated us. In the first instance, our meteorology professor trained us to accomplish a specific group of meteorology-related tasks (and at least part of the initial training had apparently failed). Our oceanography professor, however, educated us to think in a focused way about the marine environment. Both concepts are necessary. Being able to think without possessing the knowledge and skill to do any specific thing would be entirely frustrating, even useless. Being able to accomplish a specific thing—repair a car, build a house, conduct an experiment—will allow a person to survive in life and even make a meaningful contribution to society. Without the ability to think, however, to analyze cause-and-effect relationships, to understand consequences, to conceive of new relationships, people cannot long maintain a free society. History is filled with images of trained automatons marching to a dictator's drum.

Ideally, every citizen should receive an education and every citizen should be trained in one or more areas of accomplishment. At the very least, leaders in all walks of life—government, science, business, sports, entertainment, and academics—must be educated.

In the market-based school system endorsed here,

parents will naturally support the specific schools that bring to their children a proper balance of education and training. Any school failing in this regard will quickly correct its shortcomings or find itself replaced with one that works. The important thing, however, is that the parents and the community in which they live will ultimately determine the proper mix, not a top-down bureaucracy imposed from the outside.

One obvious way to produce excellence in education is to start with excellence. As a nation, we need to capture for the teaching profession those competent minds that now turn to science and industry for employment. If we create a teaching corps of brilliant achievers, we will be on our way to producing more of the same.

In life, excellence usually associates with excellence, so one order of business would be to weed out mediocre teachers, the Jimmys. We should have been able to do this with the enthusiastic cooperation of the NEA and other national teachers' organizations. Unfortunately, these organizations have endorsed tenure instead of performance as the main consideration for increased pay. Once again, they are part of the problem.

It is difficult to understand the need for a national organization that monitors the interests of teachers who are responsible to local school boards. Within the current educational framework, it seems far better to forge a local partnership among parents, teachers, and the governing boards. Even this, however, is a Band-Aid solution to a systemic problem. As with the proper balance between education and training, a market-based school system eliminates this problem as well. It seems unlikely that a national organization like the NEA could survive in a market-based school environment. When a teacher's livelihood depends on his or her ability, his or her acceptance by the parents, and the survival of his or her school, it is difficult to picture that teacher marching in a picket line. The NEA becomes irrelevant.

One of the significant problems identified in both the original study and its follow-up is that American teacher training emphasizes courses about teaching instead of knowledge courses. With the strong endorsement of the NEA, we produce a corps of teachers who know how to teach, at least in principle, but who know very little about the subjects they teach. Does anyone benefit from a math teacher with excellent teaching credentials who knows essentially nothing about fractions or long division?

In our communities live large numbers of retired people from all walks of life with many accumulated years of experience. It should be far easier to teach an experienced accountant how to transfer some of his or her knowledge to high-school kids than to teach a freshly certified high-school teacher enough accounting to have the same impact. Ditto for the retired chemist, corporate CEO, writer, mechanic, farmer . . . just about any profession or trade. The NEA's stranglehold on our public education system currently prevents all but the most persistent retirees from becoming teachers. In a market-based school system, tens of thousands of retired professional and trade people would leap at the chance to teach, probably at relatively modest salaries. This can solve the training side of the equation.

The education side, however, is more complicated. Teaching a young person to think is more challenging than teaching that person to read. Among the retired experts who can be expected to join a market-based school system will be some who ran companies, managed scientific laboratories, served as elected officials—society's leaders. They will make important contributions to the education of our children. Beyond this, however, a market-based school system can entice top-level thinkers into our basic school system as a career by offering salaries that compete with corporate America.

There is no question that our current education system is a disaster. We can continue to apply discredited top-down solutions that may produce temporary relief from or even the reversal of one or two specific problem areas. Or we can learn history's 2,500-year lesson that a successful school offers parents choice in the school, the curriculum, the teachers, and the administration and requires their financial participation in its operation.

CHAPTER 7

Government—by the Bureaucrat, for the Bureaucrat

When my father passed away in early 1987, my attorney sister and I took on the formidable task of plowing through the papers he left behind. Among them we discovered a series of letters that clearly illustrates a prevalent fact in our society.

My father was a kind and gentle man—except when it came to communicating with the IRS. His letter exchanges with that agency over the years are nothing short of astonishing. My dear father, who had a kind word for everybody, completely forgot that even the IRS is peopled with men and women who get up in the morning and put on their shoes one at a time just like you and I.

It seems that agency had not forgotten my father, for in mid-1989 it sent him a letter demanding that he pay his back taxes for 1988!

Since my father was not in a position to respond directly to this urgent request, I answered for him as follows:

IRS—Chief, Collection Branch
Philadelphia, PA 19255

Dear Sir:

I am writing you this letter to inform you that I passed away in February 1987. When my widow submitted her tax return for 1987, she had my son, whose name appears at the top of this letter, inform you that I had passed away and would, therefore, no longer be submitting income-tax returns. Since I understand that you do not have tax jurisdiction where I currently reside, I am convinced that your recent notification to me about tax delinquency (copy enclosed) is an illegal attempt to collect taxes outside of your jurisdiction, and it may even be an unconstitutional violation of the separation of church and state.

While I recognize that you have an overwhelming paperwork load, and I also understand how difficult it is these days to get competent help, I still don't believe you should be trying to collect taxes on my heavenly reward.

In light of the above, I ask (with all due respect) that you cease and desist in all further attempts to collect from me. I would hate to bring this matter to the personal attention of my superior, but if you do not leave me alone, I will have no choice.

In order to ensure that further collection attempts will not be forthcoming, would you please be good enough to send a letter to my son at the above address indicating your willingness to forgo further action. If such a letter is forthcoming, I will refrain from taking this matter up with my superior, and you may then avoid his eternal wrath—which, I understand, can be devastating.

Cordially yours, etc.

Okay—so I've had some fun at the expense of the IRS folks. I trust their day was a bit brighter. It must be tough to catch the ire of substantially everybody with whom you come in contact during the normal course of business. These people face an overwhelming task that never ends. The IRS is so large that any new technology it acquires becomes obsolete before it can be implemented. These men and women work under a heavy handicap, surrounded by thankless, hostile clients.

Congress promises no relief. Each "tax reform" only feeds the many-headed beast. Someday, our lawmakers may wake up and substitute for the income tax another, less unwieldy way to finance our government—a national value-added tax, for example, or a simple, no-deduction, flat-rate tax. I wouldn't hold my breath in anticipation, however.

Before that happens, I will probably follow my father, and the IRS can send me letters instead.

The Oxymoron of Government Efficiency

If Microsoft took ten years to implement a significant change in its computer infrastructure, it would quickly be overtaken by a hungry competitor. Granted, Microsoft does not have to process hundreds of millions of tax returns every year and, between crunch times, process a monumental incoming flow of related paperwork. Nevertheless, Microsoft does continuously process registration documents from millions of end users of its various software products, and it continuously fills its product pipeline with current software upgrades, and even new programs from time to time. The analogy isn't perfect, but there is sufficient overlap to point out that Microsoft is essentially up to date all the time, whereas the IRS never even gets its collective head above water.

I recently saw a bumper sticker that read: *If you like the post office, you will love socialized medicine.*

Point taken. The post office can't seem to move into the state-of-the-art world of modern computers any more than the IRS. Not that the post office doesn't try. Like the IRS, however, its technology implementation lags by about ten years. Think back to the PC you had on your desk ten years ago. Compare it to what you probably use today. Imagine trying to cope with that anachronism. The major mail-processing equipment used by the post office suffers similar inadequacies. By the time such equipment is put in place across the United States, and by the time it is finally operating without significant bugs, it is so outmoded that much of the internal hardware is no longer routinely available on the open market. This means, of course, that repairs are significantly more expensive than they might be were the equipment genuinely state of the art.

You can step into any other United States government agency or department and find similar situations. What's going on? Is the sky falling? Learned members of the liberal intelligentsia tell us there is no reason a government agency cannot run as efficiently as a private business. I listen to the arguments and can't help but agree: a group of dedicated government employees should be able to function with an efficiency at least as focused as a similar group working for General Electric or Ford. They never do, but they should, right?

In at least one way there is not a lot of difference between General Electric and the federal government. Both are large, unwieldy bureaucracies. In fact, one can effectively argue that from a management point of view there is only one significant difference: GE has to be profitable in order to pay its employees. Usually in commercial companies, supervisor pay is at least in part determined by the performance of the people they supervise. In any case, the long-term viability of any company is a direct function of its profitability. An employee who does not contribute in some measurable way to this profitability sooner or later will be doing something else.

When inefficiencies and actual losses reach unacceptable levels in a commercial firm, the market solves the problem. Inevitably, the bottom line rules, falling skies notwithstanding.

One can argue, however, that the very nature of government prevents bottom-line arguments from being applied. As a general rule, government consumes money. Even when government appears to be generating money, it still is a bottom-line consumer. Salaries paid to government workers, for example, ultimately derive from taxes collected from citizens, including the government workers themselves. The money put back into the economy as paid wages is always less than that taken from it through taxes. Again, it can be argued that the differential still ends up back in the economy after being used to pay for overhead and infrastructure, since eventually the money is used to pay for something, somewhere.

To illustrate this, take five individuals who earn $4,000 each, and tax them each $1,000. Use this money to pay a government worker $4,000, and use the remaining $1,000 to support the infrastructure in which this government employee works. Without the tax, the five individuals would, ideally, spend $20,000, making this money immediately available to the rest of the economy, where it will percolate through the economic system. After the tax, however, only $15,000 immediately finds its way into the economy. The remaining $5,000 is put on hold. It spends time in the collection process, in the accounting process, in the allocating process, in the payroll process, and eventually, $4,000 finds its way to the government employee and from there into the economy. The other $1,000 also eventually finds its way back into the economy.

There is a significant lag between the time the original five individuals received their money and spend it and the time the remainder of the money finally arrives in the economy. During this time, it's not doing anything. It just sits there. Like friction, it consumes economic energy without producing anything. It adds an unavoidable degree of inefficiency. A mine uses workers to extract raw material from the Earth, processes and sells the mined minerals, and uses part of the money to pay the workers and the rest to do other economic things, like investing in other operations, purchasing mining or office equipment, or whatever. A factory produces widgets that it sells for money that it uses to pay workers, purchase raw material and equipment, etc. An accounting firm sells a service, using the money to pay the accountants, purchase equipment, etc. Service firms of all kinds can profitably exist in any economy where there also exists a manufacturing base that ultimately underwrites the cost of these services. Together, production (mining, farming, etc.), manufacturing (cars, computers, etc.), and services (accounting, legal, etc.) form a synergy that keeps an entire economy afloat and working efficiently.

But wait a minute. Doesn't government supply a service, using people that it pays with taxes it collects from the consumers of that service? Isn't government part of this synergy?

Simply stated: yes, it is. A major key to the process, however, is the degree of input from each segment and the efficiency of that input. An economy that has no production or manufacturing, that consists only of services, cannot endure. There is nothing generating the underlying source of payment for the services, unless, of course, such an economy services another economy that does have a production and/or manufacturing base. Ideally, an economy will adjust so that the production and manufacturing base will balance the service sector, making everything work smoothly and efficiently.

Anytime a part of this system develops a significant inefficiency, the whole system suffers the consequences. Eventually, the inefficient element has to go, or it will drag down the entire system. For example, a manufacturing process that falls behind current technology will produce widgets that are either more expensive than gidgets, don't work as well as gidgets, or maybe are not even useful anymore, like chariot wheel spokes. If this manufacturer is subsidized with money extracted from the rest of the system, creating either an increasing but useless inventory of spokes, or tying up the money in the inefficiency of the manufacturing process, the whole system bogs down to the degree of this inefficiency. In effect, a percentage of every dollar produced in the system disappears, consumed by the friction of the inefficiency.

Fortunately, in real economic systems, chariot wheel spoke manufacturers eventually wither and die. They fall away from the whole, taking their inefficiency with them. Since this doesn't happen immediately, and since the effect exists at different levels in a whole bunch of industries and processes, every economic system has an inherent level of inefficiency that it can never overcome.

Government always adds to this inefficiency. It is inherent in the process. You cannot add a taxing entity to an economic system that consumes part of the collected taxes in overhead, and that supplies a delayed service worth less than the collected taxes, without adding a significant inefficiency burden to that system.

Sometimes the service is worth the price of the inefficiency. A good example is the military. Any economic system has to protect itself collectively from other economic systems. We need to protect ourselves from the bad guys, from the Pearl Harbors and the Twin Towers. We need a system in place to do this, and we must maintain that system. It adds inefficiency, but it cannot be avoided. It is worth the price we pay. It is clearly in our interest to make such services as efficient as possible so that the total inefficiency they add to the economy is minimized. "Lean and mean" is the goal.

On the other hand, many services government provides may not really be necessary, or they can be more efficiently accomplished within the private service sector, or there may exist a way to fund them that is much more efficient than our current tax-and-spend approach. We all benefit by eliminating needless government functions: the perpetual committee that always seems to generate another "necessary" study just as it is about to be dismantled; the agency created to solve a specific problem and, once successful, then competes with other unnecessary agencies for jurisdiction over new "problems"; and so forth for literally hundreds of government functions at the federal level and in all fifty states.

Privatizing government services that can better function in the private sector is a no-brainer. The previous chapter suggested that even the public-school system may be better off in private hands. Myriad other functions and services need to be examined in this light. The increase in efficiency gained simply by moving such functions into the private sector is phenomenal.

The Chicken Little mentality introduces another inefficiency into any system. The time and energy we exert propping up a sky that wasn't falling in the first place simply increases the friction level throughout a system.

Economist Randal O'Toole performed an in-depth study of more than 150 federal and state forest, park, wildlife, and other land and resource agencies. He examined their budgets, following their money closely. He determined the percentage of their funding originating within the budget allocation process, the user fees they collect, and where the money goes. He then evaluated the quality of their management in terms of how well they met their mandate.

As part of his analysis, O'Toole derived what he calls the *Laws of Pork and Bureaucracy.* One of the Laws of Pork, according to O'Toole, is "the most valuable pork . . . goes to the states and congressional districts of the most senior members of the Senate and House appropriations committees." Another Law of Pork is that "resorts generate more pork than grizzly bears." When the Park Service determined that a Yellowstone resort located in grizzly territory should be closed, Congress legislated that another resort had to be constructed, as it turned out, also in grizzly country. Then Congress mandated that the original resort could not be closed after all.

One of the Laws of Bureaucracy is "a bureaucracy always works to maximize its budget." As a result, excess money generated by a bureaucracy that is returned to the Treasury usually is considered a loss by that bureaucracy.

Reforming the Forest Service

Perhaps more than any other agency, the Forest Service illustrates how the Laws of Bureaucracy function.

In 1988 O'Toole published *Reforming the Forest Service,* A literary device he uses in this book is to juxtapose Lee Iacocca and an imaginary former chief of the Forest Service.

Suppose, writes O'Toole, that Lee Iacocca sells $100,000 of Chrysler stock and purchases timber stock on the advice of the former chief. A year later this investment has dropped from $50 to $30 a share, and Iacocca sells before it gets worse. I could imagine the following exchange.

"Congratulations," says the chief. "You earned $60,000."

"Sixty thousand? I started with a hundred grand; now I have only sixty—I lost forty grand."

"You don't understand," says the chief. "Your $100,000 investment doesn't count because you paid it by selling Chrysler stock."

"Actually, I lost more than forty," Iacocca bemoans. "The value of Chrysler stock increased 10 percent last year. Had I just left my money there, now I'd have a hundred-ten grand. I lost fifty, not forty grand!"

"In the Forest Service we figure it differently," answers the chief. "Since trees grow slowly, we only use 4 percent when projecting investments, so you would have earned only $4,000 had you left your money in Chrysler. Since you actually earned $60,000, you have earned fifteen times more than you would have with Chrysler."

Although this may seem like an exaggeration, this is exactly how the Forest Service projects its "profitability." Within the Forest Service, O'Toole finds a widespread attitude that timber management is cost free. Their logo says it all: "Wood is good—use it and Nature renews it." The Forest Service must consider costs, O'Toole argues, even when Nature renews the resource.

According to O'Toole, the major error in Forest Service cost accounting is the assumption that refor-estation costs are "paid for" by returns from existing timber. According to him, the Forest Service does not compare the costs of reforestation to the value of the young growth that replaces the cut timber—something the timber industry routinely does.

Forest Service "investments typically are direct refor-estation, thinnings, herbicides, fertilization, and similar tree-growth enhancing things," O'Toole writes. "Of these, only thinnings of trees with some commercial value produce income, although most of these still cost more than they produce. . . . Altogether, reforestation, precommercial thinning, herbicide release, fertilization, and the use of shade cards and other protection for seedlings may cost close to $1,000 per acre." Costs are even higher when a lot of vegetation must first be removed.

One can effectively argue that we have a national interest in preserving or replacing certain forested lands and that, in this respect, the associated costs do not matter. While this may be true, we still need to know what these costs are, in order to manage these resources efficiently. Even though it seems to consider timber management cost free, the Forest Service maximizes its budget by ignoring obvious cost-accounting principles routinely applied by the commercial timber industry. Then it uses the resulting figures to justify its inflated budget requests and takes other actions that would drive a private enterprise out of business.

Another Law of Bureaucracy is that a "bureaucracy evolves . . . through a process of natural selection whereby those people who have ideals that . . . maximize the agency's budget tend to be promoted." Thus in a surprisingly short time, people running an agency are sympathetic to the goals of the legislative funders.

O'Toole determined that our present manner of funding these agencies is completely inadequate. In fact, he says that our current funding process contributes directly to the inefficiency and poor performance of most of these agencies.

To solve this problem, he proposed that:

- agency management should be funded out of user fees, not tax dollars;
- resource agencies should be allowed to charge fair market value for their products;
- agencies should be allowed to charge for all resources in their care, not just one or a few; and
- actual agency funding should be determined by the net incomes they produce.

An agency that does not receive tax dollars immediately bypasses one of the main inefficiencies government brings to the equation. Collected tax money is not delayed in the system. Instead, just like any normal service-sector firm, such agencies collect fees for their services directly from the individuals and companies they serve.

In addition to the services they provide, many of these agencies produce one or more actual products. O'Toole suggests that they price their services and products at market, which again increases the efficiency of the entire system. Furthermore, as currently structured, many of these agencies can only charge for one or at best a small number of services or products. He suggests that agencies charge for all their services and products.

In allowing government agencies to set their own market prices, however, we must keep in mind that both the Laws of Pork and Bureaucracy still apply. We have already examined O'Toole's criticisms of Forest Service cost accounting. He also examines how the Forest Service determines prices, which clearly illustrates the need for oversight.

To illustrate the pricing process, O'Toole creates a conversation between an imaginary former chief of the Forest Service and the Chrysler governing board. To paraphrase this "conversation":

"Chrysler should sell its cars at weekly auctions held by dealers," proposes the chief.

"What if the auction prices are really low?"

"That's the advantage of this system," answers the chief. "Since most cars will be sold for some price, Chrysler won't have to worry about which car people really prefer. Of course, we will set a minimum price of $100 over the cost of transporting a replacement car to the dealer."

"That could be pretty low," comments Iacocca.

"Yes, but since the replacement car probably will sell, it may bring a higher price. If the first car were not sold, then there would be no opportunity to get this higher price."

"What about trucks?" Iacocca asks.

"We'll use a special Forest Service formula," answers the chief. "Subtract the truck operating cost from its estimated value to an average owner to obtain the residual price. We can easily outsell GMC this way."

"But will Chrysler earn money?"

"I ran the numbers through the Forest Service computer. Plymouth and Dodge will lose money, but luxury Chryslers will recoup the loss."

"Why don't we just sell those, then?"

"Americans purchased 10 million cars last year," argues the chief. "Forest Service studies show that they will agree to pay 5 percent more each year for the next ten years. Since the other manufacturers aren't gearing up for this increase, Chrysler can take advantage of it. It's important to us that all these cars be locally produced."

"It appears that the cost of the new factories you are proposing are not included in your cost-benefit analysis," observes Iacocca.

"Of course not," answers the chief. "We'll pay for most of those from last year's profits. The balance we'll amortize over fifty years because we can assume they will eventually be paid off by sale of cars."

"To sum up, then," says Iacocca, "we will lose money on most of the cars we sell, but overall we will be profitable—if we don't count capital costs."

"Exactly—just like the Forest Service has operated for fifty years."

Forest Service timber is sold at competitive auctions—proving its "fair market value," according to the Forest Service. Yet, O'Toole writes that it establishes a minimum bid that is often just fifty cents per thousand board feet plus the reforestation cost. The Forest Service justifies resulting losses, he writes, by claiming that they will be recouped from future sales of the reforested timber.

The minimum bid price for other sales—the residual price—is the value of the timber to the purchaser less the cost of logging and manufacture. O'Toole points out that this bid price frequently is less than the cost of logging and manufacture, especially outside the Pacific Northwest, which the Forest Service says is more than made up for by Pacific Northwest sales.

An old axiom says you can prove anything with numbers. It's a good thing the Forest Service has Congress for a banker.

The purpose of this discussion is to illustrate how at least one government agency uses the Laws of Pork and Bureaucracy to twist real numbers to suit its agenda. By requiring this and all other agencies to follow the previously outlined steps, all of this silliness must disappear, since real funding will depend on real numbers generated from real results.

The clincher, the suggestion that—if actually implemented—would forever change the way government is funded, will be to ensure that whatever funding an agency gets can only come from the net proceeds of its activities. At least for the kind of agencies O'Toole investigated, this guarantees their maximum efficiency, and thus the smallest possible economic impact on the overall system.

O'Toole limited his investigation to about 150 state and federal land and resource agencies. We could implement his conclusions for these agencies today. But his recommendations are applicable over a much larger range than just land and resource agencies. Practically any agency that supplies a recognized service could, in principle, be funded by the fees it charges for that service. Unfortunately, the typical user of government services is accustomed to receiving those services "for free." There are, of course, those services to "customers" who never will have the means to pay. At least in the short term, social welfare agencies and the vast assortment of services falling into this general category will have to retain traditional funding. Many services, however, such as passports or patents to name two, might be funded directly from the net proceeds of fees they could charge. The trick would be to generate a corresponding reduction in taxes, and you know how likely that would be.

Unfortunately, O'Toole's Laws of Pork and Bureaucracy will remain the driving forces of government for the foreseeable future.

Before the system changes in any significant way, I suspect my heirs will be receiving letters from outmoded IRS computers demanding that I submit my unpaid taxes. After all, everyone knows the only certain things in life are death and taxes.

CHAPTER 8
Civilized Warfare

Gen. George S. Patton once said a soldier should not strive to die for his country but rather should "make the other poor dumb bastard die for his country."

What is war? Why do we fight them? Is "civilized war" a meaningful concept? Can we realistically fight a war within a set of arbitrary rules?

Think Peace

Over the course of nearly a century, Nobel laureate Bertrand Russell tried to convince the world that violence was not an acceptable way to solve differences and that we had better options. Despite his brilliance and his passion, Russell could not effectively answer the question of what to do when attacked. His final answers seem to have been: "do nothing," and "talk if possible."

Clearly, one must survive the "do nothing" response to an attack in order to reach the "talk if possible" stage. In order for one person to survive a "do nothing" response, someone else must not do nothing—someone else must respond to the attack, fight back. When the alternative is certain death, someone has to fight.

As children attending school for the first time, we quickly learn that some children try to impose their will on those around them. When other children don't acquiesce, these little bullies initiate fights. Fortunately, higher authority in the form of a schoolteacher usually intervenes. When teacher isn't around, we learn to appease or to fight. There are no alternatives.

As we progress through school and into life, the operant higher authority changes, but it is always there. As adults in a free society, we look to the police and the courts to protect us from society's bullies. It works pretty well. Most of us go through life virtually free from physical or emotional oppression. Some members of society become victims of crime, and others are controlled by domestic violence and threats of violence, but in the final analysis, all these have recourse to the courts and—at least in principle—can receive justice.

What happens, however, when one nation is attacked by another? What happens when a Nazi Germany initiates a *Blitzkrieg* against an unsuspecting Poland, France, or Holland or a helpless Belgium? What happens when a Pearl Harbor happens?

Often in discussions like this, people get bogged down in the minutia surrounding such attacks. They start looking at motivation, provocation, retaliation, and other factors that always influence a nation's actions. When we step away from these sidetracking arguments, however, to examine the simple fact of an attack itself, what can one group of people do when attacked by another?

The Bertrand Russells of the world would have us create a higher authority such as the United Nations, subject ourselves absolutely to this authority, and then turn to this authority in the face of such an attack. They naïvely believe that the offending nation will be brought to heel by the collective moral force of the rest of the world. Unfortunately, we have learned through bitter experience that the only way to ensure our survival as a nation of free people is to be prepared to fight for that freedom.

We have no control over what an attacking enemy will use to propagate his violence. During the First World War, we discovered that using poison gas and chemical nerve agents produced unacceptable consequences. Members of the civilized world agreed never to use these agents again. But for a nation that has already demonstrated its contempt for the rule of international law by initiating an unprovoked attack, how do you stop its employment of chemical warfare?

The obvious answer is: you can't.

And so a nation must be prepared to defend against poison gas and nerve agents, even if it never intends to use them. Furthermore, in order to design an effective defense, a nation must create poison gasses, nerve agents, and other chemical horrors. And so peace-loving, freedom-loving peoples find themselves creating terrible weapons, not because they want to but because they cannot survive if they don't.

Following World War II it became clear that a determined enemy that didn't have the resources to build nuclear weapons could still create a weapon of mass destruction. By inoculating its own soldiers and people against a deadly contagious disease, and then infecting a target nation with that disease, a nation— even a small nation—can bring another to its knees.

As with chemical agents, the only way a nation can protect itself from such an attack is to create as many esoteric diseases as possible, and then develop appropriate vaccines and treatments. Once again, peace-loving, freedom-loving peoples are forced by the world's bullies to create terrible disease-causing organisms simply in order to be safe from them.

Bertrand Russell and his followers were unable to get beyond the consequences of these terrible agents. They recoiled from the horror without ever coming to grips with the awful irony that to be protected from them, we have no choice but to make them.

Preemptive Warfare

Another side of this entire argument is how to respond to an "inevitable attack" that has not yet happened, and the more complicated question of how to respond to an "attack" that has probably happened— a surreptitious strike using biologics or other forms of terror. To the first, Russell would have argued that you do nothing overt, but you talk with the firm belief that such talk inevitably will prevent the attack. This argument sounds noble, but history demonstrates that delays brought about by such talks are just that, delays, which give a potential attacker additional time to prepare.

Russell would also argue that talking early enough will prevent a surreptitious strike. No rational individual would disagree that such talks should be ongoing where possible. The important thing here, however, is that these talks must be absolutely productive, and not just a delaying tactic that allows the potential attacker to further his nefarious plans.

Waiting for an inevitable attack is as foolish as stepping into the street before a speeding car. The gunfighter mentality of the Hollywood Western, where the good guy waits for the bad guy to draw first, is movieland fantasy. It makes no sense to risk losing to a nefarious enemy, or to risk large-scale civilian casualties, when preemptive action can stop the entire situation. To the Russells, this "escalation" by the good guys is even more unacceptable than a response to an initial attack. Russell would argue that such thinking by Japan led it to attack Pearl Harbor, to stave off what Japan believed was inevitable subjugation by the United States. He would have condemned the U.S. preemptive attack against Iraq as a violation of international law.

Russell's present-day followers equate Pres. George

W. Bush with Hitler and the other evil tyrants of history, without ever understanding this simple lesson. Inevitable subjugation or death is just that: inevitable. The only way to avoid such inevitability is to destroy its agent.

These naïve people offer no viable alternative solution. Were we, as free people, to follow their counsel, we would inevitably be enslaved or killed by the tyrants waiting beyond our borders.

When the alternative is certain death, someone has to fight. If fighting sooner rather than later saves more innocent lives (read: more lives of our people), then someone has to fight preemptively.

The Soldier and the Citizen

Most people distinguish between soldiers and civilians, combatants and noncombatants. Yet history is filled with instances where one or both sides in a conflict routinely ignore this distinction. The Old Testament of the Judeo-Christian Bible gives us historic examples of battles where the victor killed everything—not just everybody, but everything: combatant soldiers, young men, old men and women, mothers and young women, children, pets, and livestock. Sometimes even the ground was salted to kill the vegetation. We have stories of indiscriminate violence perpetrated by past conquerors, from the dawn of history right up to the first notes of the modern era. But these were relatively primitive people, you might argue. They had not yet grasped the fundamental idea that human life means something.

Okay, examine the early wars between European settlers and indigenous inhabitants of North America, where the primitive natives savaged the civilized Europeans. And the civilized Europeans . . . savaged them right back, scalp for scalp, family for family, butchery for butchery. So much for "civilized."

Scan forward to relatively current times. The Nazis slaughtered millions in their death camps. We retaliated by saturation bombing German cities to piles of rubble. I saw them following the war. We left nothing standing. Uncounted thousands of civilians died. On the other side of the world, the Japanese forces slaughtered hundreds of thousands of civilians. We retaliated with Hiroshima and Nagasaki. Afterwards, during the Cold War, the Soviets slaughtered millions of civilians in Siberia. But then something began to happen in the world. Nations started taking sides on exactly this issue. In Vietnam, we went to great lengths to avoid killing noncombatants. The other side did not, and even used women and children in suicide ambushes. We prosecuted American officers and soldiers who violated this principle. In ensuing conflicts, more and more we have tried to avoid what has become known as collateral damage—the injury or death of "innocent" civilians.

"We" appear to be members of the Anglo-Japanese-European alliance: those countries comprising North America and parts of South America; Japan; Northern, Central, and Southern Europe, excluding the Balkans; Israel; South Africa; Australia and New Zealand; and some would add India.

The remainder of the world, for the most part, makes no distinction between combatants and noncombatants. This is nowhere more dramatically and terribly illustrated than the attack on the New York World Trade Center. This indiscriminate approach to battle puts those of us trying to fight in a "civilized" fashion into a quandary. Do we embrace the apparently hungry child approaching us with outstretched hands and risk being blown to bits by the hidden bomb strapped to his belly, or do we assume that every enemy child is also enemy, killing the innocent along with the guilty?

Can we afford the risk to our fundamental freedoms by saying that if you wear a turban you are the enemy? Can we afford not to?

Mutual Assured Destruction—MAD

Remember the Cold War? Step into the past, to the decades between 1950 and 1990.

In the United States, we had developed the Triad concept to protect our country—and the free world—from nuclear attack. Our defense against nuclear attack rested on three fundamentally different and independent legs.

We had a manned bomber force consisting of B-52s and B-1s. These aircraft had the obvious advantage of continuous control by humans. In an emergency the fleet could be launched and vectored by central command towards the enemy—all while frantic negotiations attempted to prevent further escalation into full-blown nuclear war. At any time, the aircraft could be recalled, or ordered not to drop their lethal loads. In the event of an escalating situation, selected bombers could be launched and maintained in a local flight pattern, continuously refueled and ready on a moment's notice to fly towards a designated target.

We had land-based Minuteman and Midgetman missiles carrying one or more independently targeted warheads with enormous explosive power. These missiles were stored in ready-to-launch hardened silos that were capable of withstanding all but a direct nuclear hit. They could knock out any potential enemy's ability to retaliate with missiles. In effect, they could pierce the enemy's hardened targets. In principle, they were capable of withstanding an enemy first strike and could then deal a devastating blow to his ability to follow through with further strikes. Missiles could be launched from these silos in a matter of minutes.

The third Triad leg was our fleet of missile submarines. These subs carried either sixteen or twenty-four missiles with multiple independently targeted warheads. The nature of submarines made it nearly impossible for a potential enemy to keep track of all our missile-bearing subs. We were, therefore, practically guaranteed to retain the ability to deliver a killing blow to any attacking enemy, even after he launched a full-blown nuclear strike against our country.

This Triad assured us the ability to deter an enemy from striking in the first place, because he could not survive such a strike.

At least, that's how it was supposed to work.

One could argue that since we did not have a nuclear war, it must have worked, and many people actually make this argument. Since the collapse of the Soviet Union, documents found in the KGB archives and reports from many former senior Soviet government personnel lend credence to this argument. The concept was called MAD, Mutual Assured Destruction. Despite the wags who could not refrain from making Dr. Strangelove analogies, MAD appears to have been very effective in deterring the Soviets from launching a nuclear strike against the United States and NATO.

The High Road—Paved with "Good" Weapons

The good news is that the Cold War is over. In response, we and the Russians have destroyed most of our land-based intercontinental ballistic nuclear missiles. Furthermore, we have severely limited the remaining two legs of the old Triad. We have retained the ability to use our bomber fleet and a limited number of ballistic missile subs to retaliate against a government with the temerity to attack us. The problem with the missile subs is that we are loath to hit a typical attacker with large nukes. Using expensive ballistic missiles to deliver anything smaller than large nukes, however, is a huge waste of money. We can do much better with high-flying bombers and smart bombs.

What options do we really have while trying to maintain the high road?

An ideal battle is one wherein only enemies die. Any weapon that nudges a battle in this direction is a "good" weapon. It is time to examine all our available options, time to erase the arbitrary line between conventional and nuclear weapons. It is time to examine what specific weapons can do, in order to evaluate their usefulness in the future battles we will face.

Why does the idea of a nuclear war frighten us so much? Nuclear war and nuclear weapons have received a bad rap. Strategic nuclear weapons serve to deter potential attackers from launching their nuclear weapons against us. Tactical nuclear weapons were developed to enable a commander faced with overwhelming odds to destroy large concentrations of enemy troops and equipment.

The mushroom cloud, since the 1950s a symbol of nuclear war, is not even a nuclear phenomenon. Any big explosion above the ground will produce a mushroom cloud. Blast, flash burn, and firestorms also are not nuclear effects. The bigger the blast—any blast—the greater the effect. The Dresden firestorm during World War II was every bit as devastating as the firestorm that engulfed Hiroshima. Nevertheless, the Dresden conflagration resulted from conventional saturation or carpet bombing, whereas the Hiroshima firestorm was the consequence of the first strategic atomic bomb explosion.

Nuclear Winter

The late Carl Sagan frightened the world with his prediction of a nuclear winter. He envisioned a post-nuclear war world wherein radioactive dust clouds raised by thousands of nuclear explosions blanketed the planet with an impenetrable cloud layer. He predicted that this cloud layer would reflect sufficient sunlight so that the planetary energy equation would fall out of balance: the Earth would radiate into space more energy that it absorbed from the sun. This would result in a centuries-long ice age and the subsequent destruction of much of the life on Earth. This scenario scared a lot of people, but it was a big, bold-faced, but very subtle lie.

Some lies are simply untrue statements. They generally are easy to refute. Display the facts, and the lie is found out. However, when you tell part of the truth but in such a fashion that it appears to be the whole truth, this sometimes is very difficult to discover. And the partial truth can lead you to a false conclusion. This is what happened with Sagan.

Scientists have constructed several mathematical models of our atmosphere. These models allow us to ask questions like: "What would happen if the atmospheric carbon dioxide level increased by 10 percent?" or "What would happen if solar output went up by one-tenth of a percent?" Since these models are simplifications of the real thing, each of them is designed to answer certain types of questions. Their ability to give meaningful answers depends on the underlying assumptions of the model and the assumptions inherent in the questions themselves.

The answers produced by these models are not exact numbers but rather a range of numbers. For example, the answer to the question about what would happen following a 10 percent increase in atmospheric carbon dioxide might be: "Average global temperature would increase by five degrees plus or minus two degrees." This means that the resulting average atmospheric temperature might increase by as much as seven degrees or as little as three degrees. Ask the same question of all the models, and you might find that the total possible range of resulting atmospheric temperature is from no change at all to an increase of ten degrees. Furthermore, even this combined, averaged result still is dependent upon the underlying assumptions. The only honest way to present the results would be to state the range and provide a framework for the underlying assumptions. Otherwise, the results would be meaningless.

Sagan used the standard atmospheric models, but he posed his questions in a way that produced the largest possible negative temperature outcomes, and then he applied his data to the extreme low end of the range of each outcome. This produced the prediction of the "nuclear winter." Granted, Sagan reported the results accurately, but he did not tell his audience that he had purposefully slanted his input data to produce the lowest possible temperatures, and he also did not explain that he chose to report only the lowest temperatures in the resulting temperature range produced by the models. He didn't say anything that was untrue; he simply did not tell the whole truth. The result was a bald-faced lie.

A nuclear explosion results when refined Uranium-235 or plutonium is suddenly jammed sufficiently close so that naturally released neutrons trigger more neutron releases, which trigger more and more. This causes a rapid buildup of pressure accompanied by an enormous release of energy—a big explosion. Normally, there is also a concurrent large, deadly release of neutrons and high-energy electrons. Explosion byproducts can remain dangerously radioactive for a long time and may be carried great distances when contained in smoke and dust—called nuclear fallout. This is the specter that nuclear weapons add to the equation of death and destruction that accompany any weapon.

The probability of a nuclear war, even a large one with thousands of explosions, producing a long-term ice age on the Earth is negligible. The cost in human lives would be appalling, but the planet would recover quickly. Radiation from fallout would be a problem, significant in some areas, only annoying in others. Modern nuclear weapons are designed to generate a large blast while producing little radioactive residue. The idea is to destroy or significantly damage the enemy's missile silos and other means of retaliation. There is no benefit in hitting population centers or in spreading radioactive dust.

Tactical Nukes

With the demise of the Soviet Union as a world superpower, the risk of worldwide nuclear war has nearly vanished. Global stockpiles of strategic nuclear weapons, the kind of weapons Sagan envisioned in his misbegotten scenario, are dramatically reduced. The nuclear weapons we still have, the ones that might yet find their place on a modern battlefield, are tactical devices.

Tactical nuclear devices fall into three categories: low yield, neutron, and portable. Low-yield tactical shells allow a commander to eliminate a large emplacement of equipment and infrastructure. One shell can put a lot of equipment out of commission. One "small" bomb can flatten an entire building complex. Perhaps of more significance in today's antiterrorist battle, a tactical warhead on a burrowing device can destroy a large underground complex in one fell swoop. It would be like exploding one or two million pounds of TNT a hundred feet below the surface near or in an underground complex of tunnels and caves. It gets the job done.

A neutron device substantially reduces nuclear-blast effect while significantly increasing initial release of high-energy neutrons and electrons, and it practically eliminates any consequent nuclear fallout. The result is little or no blast damage, nearly total destruction of human and animal life within the burst radius, and no residual effects at all. Using such a neutron device, a commander can eliminate enemy troops, while leaving their equipment, structures, the landscape, and the environment essentially intact. For most of the enemy troops, death is practically instantaneous, although for those in outlying areas of the burst radius, death, while just as certain, will be slower.

Is this cruel and unusual? Is this inhumane, uncivilized? Compare the lingering death of a soldier with both legs and half his stomach blown away by a grenade to the swift death of a soldier exposed to a pulse of deadly high-energy neutrons. Dead is dead, but the agony experienced by the grenade-wounded soldier is infinitely greater than the relatively swift death of the soldier exposed to the neutron device. The soldier exposed to a lower level of neutrons still faces probable death, but—unlike the lingering grenade death—he will die with comparatively little pain.

When individual weapons are viewed more dispassionately, tactical neutron devices become more like conventional high-kill battlefield weapons and much less like strategic, high-yield thermonuclear bombs. Their use can then not only be tolerated, but encouraged as a way to reduce our own battlefield deaths—our fathers, sons, and brothers—without the specter of "nuclear holocaust."

The SADM

SADM is military jargon for Special Atomic Demolition Munitions. It is a fifty-eight-pound "back-pack nuke" with about 250 times the explosive strength of the bomb that killed American Marines in Lebanon.

In the hands of American Special Operations commandos like the Army Rangers, Special Forces, Marine Recon, and Navy Seals, these little devices can be placed behind enemy lines to take out strategic targets like dams, power plants, bridges, etc. This can be done surreptitiously before actual conflict, with the devices set to be activated by remote signal. Because there will be no telltale aircraft, no missile contrails, no revealing emissions, the enemy will have no advance notice of the loss of these facilities. One moment the dam is there; the next it isn't.

Fuel-Air Explosives—FAE

Even though tactical nukes seem "ideal" under many circumstances, there often are overriding political and ethical considerations. When weapons are divided into only two categories—conventional and nuclear—the problem devolves into who will employ nukes first. This is unfortunate, because the answer usually will be to refrain from using all nukes. In the face of overwhelming odds, resulting friendly troop deaths will escalate dramatically.

Certain battlefield conditions seem to demand using tactical nuclear devices. Unfortunately, political considerations may override the arguments presented here, precluding their use. Fuel-Air Explosives or FAE technology bypasses the "limitations" of nuclear devices. An FAE weapon produces an explosion rivaling a tactical nuclear blast. Fill the air above a target with an explosive mixture of fuel, and then ignite it all at once. When done properly, using the right fuel mixture, this produces an explosion functionally equivalent to one or two millions pounds of TNT. An FAE weapon leaves behind complete devastation, every bit equal to that resulting from a tactical nuke, although the total explosive energy is a lot less. The origin of the explosive energy in a tactical nuke is a point source: the shell or bomb. The explosive energy released from a fuel-air explosion is distributed over the entire area of the explosive fuel mixture. Thus significantly different total energies can produce essentially equivalent results. Furthermore, fuel-air explosions produce no residual radioactivity.

Another effect of the FAE is characterized by its Russian nickname: Vacuum Bomb. Because the explosion rapidly consumes all available oxygen within a sphere with a radius of approximately three hundred yards, the explosion sucks oxygen towards it so rapidly that it leaves a surrounding deadly vacuum. The effect of this vacuum, especially in conjunction with a fuel-air explosion on or near a cave and tunnel complex, is devastating. Nothing can survive.

FAE deployment requires the ability to deliver a fairly large container to the desired location and keep it there long enough to expel the explosive mixture. The explosion must be initiated before the fuel cloud can disperse. This usually is accomplished by deploying a container with two fuses, where the first fuse initiates the fuel dispersion and the second, delayed fuse initiates the actual explosion. The most recent implementation of the FAE is a 15,000-pound, automobile-sized container parachuted to the site from an appropriate aircraft and detonated by remote control.

A Clear Choice

When the alternatives are hand-to-hand combat while outnumbered five-to-one by battle-hardened enemy soldiers, or using tactical nukes to destroy those soldiers without significant risk to friendly troops, the choice should be clear. It is high time we abandoned outmoded thinking about "nuclear" weapons as categorically different from "conventional" weapons, and placed our complete arsenal at the disposal of field commanders.

Patton really did have the right idea: make the other poor dumb bastard die for his country.

CHAPTER 9

The Anatomy of a Nuke

The bad news is that we have ballistic missile subs floating around, but there really is nothing they can effectively deter. September 11, 2001, lies behind us. The missile subs, and our fleet of bombers for that matter, clearly did not deter anything.

For deterrence to work, you must know where a strike would originate—something quite easy to determine when the enemy uses missiles or military attack aircraft. In the wake of the destruction of the New York World Trade Center, we face something completely different.

We are able to make effective use of our bomber fleet to combat terrorism, but fleet ballistic missile subs still have only one purpose, to deter nuclear-armed, would-be opponents from launching a preemptive nuclear strike against us. We don't have as many of these subs as in the past, but we still have an effective fleet of hidden and essentially unstoppable vehicles capable of totally destroying any nation choosing to attack us. As such, it still deters.

The Nuclear Posture Review

On March 10, 2002, the *Los Angeles Times* and the *New York Times* reported the release of a secret Pentagon paper presenting the findings of the second Nuclear Posture Review (NPR). According to both newspapers, this report is a comprehensive plan for developing and deploying nuclear weapons. The newspaper coverage purported to reveal controversial information about the NPR that captured the imagination of world leaders and generated significant negative reaction towards the United States from around the world.

It is surprising that these eminent newspapers only reported on this development on March 10, since the actual paper was disseminated to the press back on January 9 by J. D. Crouch, the assistant secretary of defense for international security policy, with the active participation of Rear Adm. Barry M. Costello, deputy director for strategy and policy on the joint staff; John Harvey, director, Office of Policy, Planning, Assessment and Analysis for the Department of Energy; and Richard McGraw, principal deputy assistant secretary of defense for public affairs.

McGraw led off the January 9 briefing with some general remarks alluding to the first Nuclear Posture Review completed in 1994. This review was a response to the dramatically altered world following the collapse of the Soviet Union and the end of the Cold War. It created an operating framework for this changed situation.

Crouch then presented fifteen slides that outlined the findings of the current Nuclear Posture Review. This was followed by questions from the press answered by one or more of the participants.

While it is true that portions of the review are classified, the reasons for this were clearly stated in the briefing. Crouch and his assembled experts answered questions about these reasons and went into significant detail about the motivations for and findings of the review.

A cover letter from Defense Secretary Donald H. Rumsfeld had been sent to Congress and was handed out at this briefing. Rumsfeld explained that the

Nuclear Posture Review was built on the 2001 Quadrennial Defense Review (QDR) ordered by President Bush. The QDR and NPR together, he wrote, put in place a major change in approach to the role of nuclear defensive forces in U.S. deterrent strategy, and present the blueprint for transforming our strategic policy.

He went on to write that the NPR establishes a New Triad composed of (1) offensive strike systems (both nuclear and non-nuclear); (2) defenses (both active and passive), and (3) a revitalized defense infrastructure that will provide new capabilities in a timely fashion to meet emerging threats.

He then explained that the New Triad was designed both to reduce our dependence on nuclear weapons, and improve our ability to deter attack in the face of proliferating weapons of mass destruction (WMD) capabilities by (1) the addition of defenses, reducing our reliance on offensive strike forces; and (2) the addition of non-nuclear strike forces, reducing our reliance on nuclear strike forces.

In several articles breathlessly echoed by broadcast and cable news networks, both newspapers then reported that the United States had taken a dramatic turn towards a war footing. They reported that the list of potential nuclear targets had expanded to include Iraq (this was prior to the war), Iran, North Korea, Syria, and Libya, engendering a flood of protest and invective from these countries and their friends.

Contrary to what has been reported, the first leg of the New Triad—the offensive leg—will go beyond a reduced level of the Cold War trio of intercontinental ballistic missiles (ICBMs), sea-launched ballistic missiles (SLBMs), and manned bombers to include new non-nuclear strike weapons and newly developed, lower-yield nukes. This will dramatically strengthen the credibility of our strategic deterrence.

The second leg of the New Triad, recognizing the impact of 9/11, requires development of both active and passive defenses that will deny or reduce the effectiveness of limited attacks, and so discourage those attacks. This leg will also "provide new capabilities for managing crises, and provide insurance against the failure of traditional deterrence," according to Rumsfeld.

The third leg is a responsive defense infrastructure. It will address our ability to bring new weapons on line and will reshape our nuclear infrastructure. This will make us far less reliant upon large, strategic nuclear weapons and better able to deploy tactical weapons that pose a much smaller threat to the world at large. These smaller weapons will also give us the ability to hold off massed armies that might otherwise be able to overrun our forces. Furthermore, maintaining our flexible response capability to large strategic changes can positively dissuade potential adversaries from developing WMDs.

The New Triad's effectiveness depends on "command and control, intelligence, and adaptive planning," according to Rumsfeld. He proffered the term "exquisite" intelligence to describe where we are headed. Such advance knowledge of the capabilities and intentions of our potential adversaries will give us the ability to adjust the degree of force we will use and the precision of how we will use it. No longer will we stand with a huge nuclear hammer raised to obliterate a potential foe.

Instead, we will have the ability to strike where it will hurt the most, pulling the plug on an offender before he is able to carry out any threats. Having already demonstrated this ability to some degree in Afghanistan, and convincingly in Iraq, we now can cast our antiterrorist glance more effectively at other offending nations. It may even be that a glance alone will suffice to solve many extant problems.

The NPR raises a particularly interesting point. Can

a modern "smart" conventional weapon outperform a nuke, and so obviate the need for that particular nuke?

In my submarine days, we carried several torpedoes. One was the Mark 45, a nuke with an underwater kill radius of about one cubic mile of ocean. In other words, if your submarine was anywhere within a half-mile of the burst—in any direction—you were dead meat. We also carried the Mark 37, which was a "smart" torpedo—not so smart as the torpedoes used today but still plenty bright. These "fish" used sonar sensing and tracking abilities. They also had a kill radius of about a cubic mile. Because they were not nukes, however, they were much easier to handle, easier on the guys—including less paperwork!—and less dangerous for the sub, since we had more control over what and where it could strike, and so could stay within the kill zone and still be safe. The Mark 45 absolutely mandated that we be outside the kill zone.

In many cases, a modern smart weapon may very well be a better weapon than a tactical nuke. This is especially true for weapons utilized to wipe out specific units, vehicles, or complexes. Unless the complex is heavily reinforced or well fortified underground, a smart weapon probably will be a better choice than a nuke.

The NPR specifically recommends developing a better burrowing nuke for wiping out deeply fortified cave-like complexes. Other than this recommendation, the report is silent on what might be forthcoming. It just leaves the door open for future development.

One wonders, therefore, at what motivated the *New York Times* and the *Los Angeles Times* to shout so loudly about a report that was released over two months prior to their articles. One wonders how they managed to distort the NPR into a warmongering document, when it actually paves the way towards a more peaceful world, less likely to become involved in a planetary nuclear war.

On the other hand, since these newspapers also reported as straight news the Doomsday Clock movement by the left-wing *Bulletin of the Atomic Scientists*, perhaps a hidden agenda is peeking out from under their self-righteous indignation.

The Doomsday Clock

The following news release appeared shortly after a *Time* magazine article about the possibility that al Qaeda had gained possession of a ten-kiloton nuclear device: "Chicago, February 27, 2002: Today, the Board of Directors of the *Bulletin of the Atomic Scientists* moves the minute hand of the 'Doomsday Clock,' the symbol of nuclear danger, from nine to seven minutes to midnight, the same setting at which the clock debuted fifty-five years ago. Since the end of the Cold War in 1991, this is the third time the hand has moved forward."

Since 1949, the hands on this clock have moved eighteen times. In 1953 the *Bulletin* set the clock at two minutes to midnight, and in 1991, with the collapse of the Soviet Union, they backed the clock to seventeen minutes before midnight. Since then it has moved closer three times, to its present position of seven minutes before midnight.

The position of the "Doomsday Clock" has always been big news. Its movement never fails to capture the public's imagination, especially when it is towards rather than away from midnight. After all, newsmakers and reporters and public leaders reason, "Atomic scientists surely know whereof they speak."

Right?

Well, probably—if it were actually atomic scientists doing the speaking, and if they were speaking about atomic weapons, about which they probably know a great deal.

So who are these folks alarming the world while posing as "atomic scientists"?

For starters, their real name is the Educational Foundation for Nuclear Science (EFNS), formed in Chicago in 1949 as a nonprofit organization. They are currently sponsored by—read, "these are people who allow their names to appear on their letterhead"—a group of thirty-nine eminent men of science and letters, including twelve Nobel laureates. They also list twenty-six deceased scientists and academics, including another fourteen Nobel laureates.

This is pretty impressive, so long as you don't probe beneath the surface to discover who actually decides *Bulletin* editorial policy, the EFNS organizational point of view, and the all-important Doomsday Clock position. The governing board consists of fifteen people, nearly all from well-known intellectual groups holding political points of view ranging from the left to the far left. A partial listing includes the Union of Concerned Scientists, Physicians for Social Responsibility, Program on Global Security and Disarmament, Institute for International Peace Studies, and Peace Research Institute Frankfurt.

These folks have a clear, well-defined agenda, one that—more often than not—is opposed to the official position of the U.S. government and—more importantly—represents an outlook inherently bad for us, the citizens of the United States.

Hiding behind the guise of "atomic scientists," these hard-core members of the intellectual left inject fear and panic into the social context every time they move their ominous clock nearer midnight.

Safeguarding Nukes

Having nuclear-armed missile subs floating around

the ocean, however, raises an interesting and important question: Could a ballistic missile submarine commander launch his missiles without specific presidential authorization? Could a few men conspire and successfully bypass the built-in safety systems to launch nuclear weapons?

The people who established our nuclear weapons control systems fully understood the omnipresent element of human uncertainty. To offset this, they created the Reliability Program.

Anybody with access to any element of nuclear weapons is under continuous, close scrutiny. From the admiral in command of a flotilla to the least significant seaman swabbing the deck around the outside of a missile tube—every individual having even the remotest contact with nuclear weapons and their means of delivery participates in the most closely supervised "buddy system" in the world.

Every participating individual submits to a background investigation. Its depth depends on the individual's ultimate responsibilities and potential for causing a problem. Before being assigned to more sensitive positions, individuals' dossiers must be updated, with the level of any additional investigation appropriately intensified.

Beyond this, however, each individual is specifically and legally responsible for observing every other individual in the program with whom he or she comes into contact.

If Lieutenant Jones suddenly starts drinking three cups of coffee in the morning instead of just one, Seaman Smith, who brings him the coffee, must report this change. If he doesn't, and if this change and Smith's knowledge of this change become factors in a future problem, Smith will suffer consequences as severe as Jones. This system has worked since the early 1960s.

Every element that is remotely connected with launch authorization is under continuous "two-man control." It takes two individuals to bring together any system element that can ultimately lead to the launch of a nuclear weapon. These individuals, while they usually will know each other, are prohibited from establishing close personal ties. In the event that such ties happen, they must voluntarily step forward with this information and be reassigned. Failure to do this requires their dismissal and disciplinary action.

Only the president can authorize a nuclear weapons launch. His authorization will arrive at the submarine by secure radio, encoded by long-established, reliable methods. To ensure that the message is authentic, sealed authenticators are used. Created and distributed under continuous two-man control and with the tightest security available to modern technology, each set of these authenticators contains identical symbols, entirely unknown to anybody. They are created automatically by computers programmed to insert completely random symbols. To further safeguard their integrity, on a moment's notice, sets are randomly invalidated system-wide.

A launch message identifies a specific authenticator and lists the symbol it should contain. This symbol will have been determined by the sender only moments before transmitting the message by manually opening one of the authenticators. If the local authenticator does not match, the message is not authenticated, and the launch is denied. Authenticators can be used only once and are handled with the strictest control of anything in the military command and control system. The Reliability Program ensures the integrity of the authentication step to the limits of human capability. The mindset of the people entrusted with authenticator control and missile launch is totally suffused with the precepts of the Reliability Program.

As the communications officer on one of these subs, I remember being summoned to the comm shack (the radio room) by a general announcement to meet the executive officer so we together could open the authenticator safe, each using our secret, personal combination code. My senior chief radioman stood directly behind us at parade rest. He was armed with a standard-issue, .45-caliber semiautomatic pistol. Before we arrived in the comm shack, the chief had chambered a round. His holster was unsecured. I had no doubt that he could draw and fire before either the XO or I could overpower him. We were all in the Reliability Program. That's how it worked then, and how it works now.

The likelihood of three or four individuals conspiring to bypass this system is extremely remote. While one can easily imagine two officers and the communications chief petty officer colluding in this way, when one sets up the actual logistics of such a collusion, it is practically impossible. In order for these individuals to commence a conspiracy after being assigned to the sub, all three would have to be failures of the Reliability Program. One can conceive of one such failure, or even two or three, but for all three to find themselves on the same nuclear submarine at the same time is a high-order statistical improbability. To set up such a collusion using moles would require such intimate knowledge and control of the entire navy personnel-assignment system, such wholesale penetration of nearly every branch of the navy, as to render this virtually impossible.

A presidential "shadow" carries the currently active authenticator set and several backups—always under two-man control. Should the president and his immediate staff be lost, the entire system can rapidly shift to the next responsible official so that within minutes appropriate launch messages can be authenticated— using another set of authenticators.

Is there a way to launch a nuclear weapon by accident? Can a specific accidental series of events take place—no matter how remote—that will result in the inevitable launch or detonation of a nuclear weapon?

We already know that one individual working alone or several individuals working in collusion cannot realistically bring about the deliberate launch of a nuclear weapon by somehow bypassing the authenticator controls or overcoming the Reliability Program.

What about causing an unprogrammed launch or a local nuclear detonation?

We are protected from unprogrammed launching of nuclear weapons by mechanical safeguards and by carefully structured and controlled mandatory procedures that are always employed when working around nuclear weapons.

Launching a nuclear weapon takes the specific simultaneous action of several designated individuals. System designers ensured that conditions necessary for a launch could not happen accidentally.

For example, to launch a missile from a ballistic missile submarine, two individuals must insert and turn keys into separate slots on separate decks within a few seconds of each other. Barring this, the system cannot physically launch a missile. There are additional safeguards built into the system that control computer hardware and software, and personnel controls we discussed earlier. In the final analysis, however, without the keys inserted as described, there can be no launch—it's not physically possible. Because the time window for key insertion is less than the physical time required for one individual to move between the two key positions, it is physically impossible for a missile to be launched by one individual. Any launch must be deliberately accomplished by at least two people.

Maintenance procedures on nuclear weapons are very tightly controlled. The "two-man control" rule always is in effect. This rule prohibits any individual from accessing nuclear weapons or their launch vehicles alone. At least two individuals always must be present. No matter how familiar the two technicians may be with a specific system, each step in a maintenance procedure is first read by one technician, repeated by the second, acknowledged by the first (or corrected, if necessary), performed by the second, examined by the first, checked off by the first, and acknowledged by the second. This makes maintenance slow, but absolutely assures that no errors happen.

Exactly the same procedure is followed every time an access cover is removed, a screw is turned, a weapon is moved, or a controlling publication is updated. Nothing, absolutely nothing, is done without following the written guides exactly, always under two-man control. This even applies to guards. Where nuclear weapons are concerned, a minimum of two guards—always fully in sight of each other—stand duty.

One can postulate a scenario wherein a technician bypasses the mechanical safeguards in order to effect a launch by himself. Technically, such a deliberate launch would be possible, but we have already determined the extraordinary unlikelihood of this happening. While one can conceive of one rogue technician slipping through the Reliability Program, in order for this technician to accomplish the modifications to allow a single-person launch, it would absolutely require the collusion of at least one other person. There is no realistic way one person could spend the necessary time alone with the launch system to effect such a modification. The chance of this, as we have seen, is astronomically remote.

There is no realistic scenario wherein a nuclear missile can be accidentally or deliberately launched without authorization . . . ever . . . under any circumstances . . . period! The system isn't foolproof, but within the limitations of the trust we place in our highest officials, it nearly eliminates the chance of a nuclear weapon being launched without proper authority.

We have established a credible need for a nation to create a military, since without the means to protect itself, a nation cannot survive. We have explored the implications of chemical and biological weapons and why even a peaceful people cannot avoid developing such weapons, if only to create adequate defenses against them. We have examined the continuing need for nuclear weapons and their safekeeping.

It is completely obvious why we take special precautions to safeguard chemical and biological weapons. It may seem equally obvious why we go to such lengths to protect nuclear weapons, but it is worth spending some time examining our understanding and our assumptions.

Surreptitious Importation Strike—SIS

In today's post-Cold War world, conventional warfare no longer occupies central stage. Enter the surreptitious importation strike (SIS). It's a phrase coined in the mid-1980s by Charles Harrison, writing in the *Mensa Bulletin*. Modern warfare no longer is just large armies facing one another across battle lines, fighting ships in ferocious sea battles, or even exchanging intercontinental ballistic missiles from opposite sides of the Earth. Since September 11, 2001, SIS has become terribly real and immediate. Terrorism has become the biggest threat to life, liberty, and happiness. Its ugly implications are overwhelming: anthrax attacks and attacks on the New York World Trade Center, the Pentagon, the USS *Cole*, our embassies around the world . . .

SADMs are so small that they can go anywhere a man can. Should they find their way into the hands of terrorists, Mafia thugs, enemy infiltrators, or even several disgruntled nuclear-lab technicians, it will be entirely possible one day to discover that major industrial and cultural centers throughout our country have been blanketed with these devices. They would be nearly impossible to locate, would remain potent for years, and can be activated by a simple coded radio command from almost anywhere.

Fortunately, SADM-like devices are very difficult to build. Even with actual plans in hand, most organized groups would not be able to produce the final product. In fact, good evidence indicates that the Communist Chinese government held complete SADM plans for ten years without being able to construct a working model, despite their relatively sophisticated technology. We can, therefore, discount the chance that a terrorist group will be able to build its own SADM devices in the near future.

Realistically, anyone wanting SADM devices must resort to theft. Our defense against SADM attacks, therefore, is absolute control of SADMs in the first place.

We know the location of all our SADMs, and we keep them under strictest possible control, with essentially zero chance that one could fall into enemy hands. We believe the Soviets developed similar devices but suspect theirs lack our sophisticated miniaturization. Because of the disruption following the demise of the Soviet Union, a terrorist organization might be able to obtain one of the Soviet portable nukes, but it appears unlikely that they could detonate the device—at least, not without outside expertise. The task is formidable, but not impossible.

What about terrorists gaining possession of one of the larger nuclear warheads from the former Soviet Union?

The February 2002 *Time* magazine article revealed a report by an informant, Dragonfly, that terrorists might have taken possession of a ten-kiloton Soviet nuclear warhead. Media reports carried the *Time* assertions that such a weapon exploded in Times Square would flatten everything inside a radius of half a mile, kill 100,000 people outright, and irradiate another 700,000. A Fox News reporter breathlessly explained that this bomb would leave a mile-wide hole in the ground.

Assuming that the weapon *Time* reported on is real (and setting aside the question of whether or not al Qaeda terrorists actually got one), and that it really has an explosive yield of about ten kilotons, then it probably came from one of the old Soviet Multiple Independently Targeted Reentry Vehicle (MIRV) missiles. The Hiroshima bomb was about thirteen kilotons, but it was a very large, clumsy fission device. In order to make a ten-kiloton bomb sufficiently small to fit into a missile payload bay along with another nine or ten bombs, they all must be tritium-boosted thermonuclear devices—little hydrogen bombs.

Tritium-boosted devices work like this. You first construct a sphere about the size of and sectioned like a soccer ball, with the individual sections consisting of weapons-grade plutonium. Next, you attach an explosive charge to each of the sections, fill the sphere with tritium (a radioactive form of hydrogen), and seal it so that nothing escapes.

To detonate the device, you set off the explosive charges simultaneously, so that all the plutonium meets forcefully at the center of the sphere. There it commences a fission (atomic bomb) explosion, which in turn causes the tritium to undergo a fusion reaction, and presto—you have a hydrogen- or thermonuclear-bomb explosion. By modifying the firing sequence of the explosive charges, you can vary where inside the sphere the fission explosion happens. This results in a specific shape to the explosion, so that it delivers more of its energy at the target and less to the surrounding environment.

This detonation process requires extraordinary accuracy. Any failure to meet the weapon's precise design parameters will leave you with—literally—a pop and a fizzle. Furthermore, tritium is a very sneaky gas. It can slip through solid steel; it can escape like Houdini from any confinement. Nothing, absolutely nothing, can retain tritium over the long haul. The U.S. weapons program continuously recharges the tritium in its boosted weapons, because the darn stuff simply leaks out, goes away, vanishes.

The Soviet Union collapsed in 1991. Any weapon held by terrorists would be at least that old. By now, any remaining tritium inside the sphere has certainly vanished like the value of Enron stock. Based on my analysis of current terrorism and nuclear weapons technology, I can say that no terrorist organization in the world has the ability to generate sufficient tritium to recharge one of these devices.

Even if they could recharge the device with tritium, they still are more likely to get a poof than a bang. It is highly unlikely that such a weapon could have been transported around since 1991 without suffering sufficient jarring and incidental damage to make the firing sequence totally unreliable.

What if they actually could make the weapon work?

In the first place, such a weapon is designed to explode high above the target in what weapon designers call an air-burst detonation. The force of the explosion is directed downwards like a giant fist, crushing everything beneath it and irradiating everything inside a broad cone. Al Qaeda terrorists simply lack the means to make it happen this way.

At best, they could transport the device to the top of a skyscraper for detonation. More realistically, they would have to explode it at some intermediate level. There is no way these guys can get the device to any level higher than fifteen or twenty floors, but even this is unlikely. The only genuinely realistic scenario is a near-ground burst from inside a residential building.

Three months after the *Time* magazine article appeared, the *New York Times Magazine* featured an 8,000-word cover story by staff reporter Bill Keller entitled "Nuclear Nightmares." I first heard about this article on an early-morning public-radio interview with Keller broadcast over KPCC out of Pasadena City College, northeast of Los Angeles. The short interview focused on the last few paragraphs of Keller's article, wherein he reported the results of a computer model created by Dr. Matthew McKinzie, a staff scientist at the Natural Resources Defense Council (NRDC).

Natural Resources Defense Council—NRDC

It is quite useful to understand just who McKinzie and the NRDC really are. The NRDC is a Washington, D.C.-based environmental group that claims approximately half a million members worldwide and a staff of "respected scientists, lawyers, and environmental specialists." It has offices in New York, Washington, Los Angeles, and San Francisco.

In fact, the NRDC is a left-wing organization that has been trying to eliminate anything nuclear since its inception in 1970. Dr. McKinzie was initially a researcher at Los Alamos. Apparently his left-wing politics led him to get caught up in the so-called "international peace movement" that was surreptitiously promoted and funded by the international communist movement of that period, and he ended up as a "staff scientist" with the NRDC. At the NRDC, McKinzie focused on generating computer programs that purport to demonstrate the effects of nuclear explosions on civilian populations and municipal infrastructures.

Although I have not had the opportunity to examine McKinzie's specific computer models, physics is a two-way street. One can start with a set of conditions, apply them to a mathematical model that contains certain assumptions, and generate a result based upon those conditions, the assumptions, and the math and physics contained in the model. Or one can start with a result, apply both the original conditions and the underlying math and physics, and from this one can generate the assumptions used in the model.

This "reverse engineering" approach has its pitfalls, since the math and physics one applies, while certainly one of the constants in this problem, can be from one of several basic approaches to the original problem. Nevertheless, it is quite possible, with very little effort, to zero in on the basic assumptions McKinzie has used in his models.

Another interesting point about McKinzie and the NRDC is that he has been applying these models to various scenarios as requested by other members of the anti-nuclear left: to studies in Canada, in Pakistan, and elsewhere. Always with the same message: nuclear is bad. The predicted results presented by McKinzie and his fellow travelers are always horrific, always unthinkable, always obvious justification for doing away with anything nuclear.

Time magazine probably used one of McKinzie's ten-kiloton models to generate its reckless and inaccurate prediction of a half-mile radius of destruction, 100,000 people dead and another 700,000 irradiated. Here is McKinzie's predicted one-kiloton result, taken directly from Keller's article:

> The blast and searing heat would gut buildings for a block in every direction, incinerating pedestrians and crushing people at their desks. Let's say 20,000

dead in a matter of seconds. Beyond this, to a distance of more than a quarter mile, anyone directly exposed to the fireball would die a gruesome death from radiation sickness within a day—anyone, that is, who survived the third-degree burns. This larger circle would be populated by about a quarter million people on a workday. Half a mile from the explosion, up at Rockefeller Center and down at Macy's, unshielded onlookers would expect a slower death from radiation. A mushroom cloud of irradiated debris would blossom more than two miles into the air, and then, 40 minutes later, highly lethal fallout would begin drifting back to earth, showering injured survivors and dooming rescue workers. The poison would ride for 5 or 10 miles on the prevailing winds, deep into the mushroom cloud or Queens or New Jersey.

Here is how McKinzie arrived at these results. First, he assumed that the area surrounding the explosion had a certain population density. Whatever exact figure he used, I have no quarrel with the number; I am certain it was in the ballpark. Then he assumed a blast effect calculated from previous experiments, most accomplished in the 1950s at the Nevada test site. He probably modified these results to account for more modern technology, and since none of these tests was ever performed on such a small device, he modified his assumptions to accommodate this fact.

I take issue with several parts of this process. The measurements made in the 1950s were taken at a significant distance from the blasts. They were made with equipment that was relatively primitive by today's standards. The explosive devices were crude by today's standards, and there really is no way to extrapolate the results of these explosions to what happens with a modern one-kiloton device. Furthermore, these measurements were made across a flat expanse of desert, not in a city environment surrounded by substantial high-rise buildings.

This really is the key. If you take the simple results from the 1950s tests, extrapolate them down to one kiloton, and apply the results to the presumed population distributed across a half-mile radius, the results will be very much like what McKinzie predicted.

The moment you insert dozens of substantial buildings, however, most of concrete and steel construction, the entire problem changes radically. The force of any blast is transmitted through the air—no air, no blast effect, despite what you see on sci-fi flicks. As this spherical cauldron expands during the first microseconds, almost immediately it encounters very dense walls of steel-reinforced concrete. The closest buildings will not be gutted so much as destroyed. The heat probably will vaporize sufficient material at the bases of these buildings to cause them to collapse.

Considering just the damage without the blast, the buildings probably would collapse inwards, tilting towards the center. In our scenario, however, a portion of the blast will be funneled upwards, somewhat like a chimney, expanding as it rises. This will counter the inward-falling tendency, so that the buildings will tend to fall into their footprint. It may also be that some of the taller buildings will actually be forced outwards by the rising blast.

By the second or third layer of buildings, the blast will have been substantially absorbed in the horizontal plane. The rising blast plume will certainly affect the buildings' upper floors, but the buildings in direct contact with the blast are goners anyway.

Of course, the people in the immediate vicinity will be killed. But if you are two or three buildings away, especially if these buildings are substantial, you may not even be hurt by the blast.

There will be an initial flood of neutrons, and they will kill if they go through you, even if you are a mile away. Thus, along the thoroughfares directly exposed to the blast, there will be some serious radiation damage, and they may also funnel the blast to a greater distance as well. The several layers of reinforced-concrete buildings will stop the neutrons in other directions. Immediately following the neutrons will be gamma (high-energy photons) and beta (high-energy electrons) radiation. The gamma will also funnel along the thoroughfares but with considerably less damage. It will be completely absorbed by the first layer of concrete. As we learned in chapter 3, beta can be stopped by a few inches of air or your skin. Unless you are directly exposed to a great deal, beta will cause no problem. Alpha is really not radiation at all but helium nuclei. It is only dangerous if actually taken inside the body. Typically, it is present in the fallout from a nuclear explosion.

So far we have some pretty serious damage out to maybe three buildings and along the exposed thoroughfares. We have some radiation damage from neutrons and gamma along the same thoroughfares, and some localized beta damage.

The fallout is totally dependent upon the kind of explosion—basically, how dirty it was. Small nukes are specially designed to be very clean, that is, without any major radiation aftereffects. Thus, the blast plume that shoots up through the buildings will be relatively clean; it will contain few alpha-producing substances.

The bottom line is that such a bomb exploded on a typical New York street corner (Times Square in Keller's example) will not produce anywhere near the level of damage predicted by McKinzie. In fact, the ten-kiloton bomb in the *Time* magazine article will not produce the kind of damage he predicted!

So much for NRDC science.

Keller opened his article with an account of a conversation he had with Russian nuclear physicist Vladimir Shikalov. Shikalov, who had participated in the Chernobyl cleanup following the 1986 reactor accident, described a possible terrorist scenario where about a cup of radioactive Cesium-137 would be surreptitiously sprayed into the air inside Disneyland. Keller estimated that this action probably would shut down the place for good and constitute a "staggering strike at Americans' sense of innocence."

Shikalov believes—correctly—that most people are irrationally afraid of radiation. He indicated that he would have no problem visiting Disneyland following such an attack. He thought he might carry his own food and drink and destroy his clothing afterwards, as a general safety precaution, but he firmly believes that Americans' fear of radiation would push us to an extreme reaction to such an attack.

To his credit, Keller included this story in his article, but he soon abandoned its common-sense view for more extreme anti-nuclear ones like McKinzie's. I responded to Keller's article in some detail on the *New York Times* discussion board linked to the article on the Internet. In response, I received an email from which I have extracted the following passage, which speaks for itself:

> Your article, posted as a link from the *New York Times Magazine* cover story, was the only reason I got to sleep last night. 1) Thank you. 2) Do you feel that fears are being exaggerated in general? What is the reason the media/govt is doing this? 3) I live in New York and am scared s---less.

The Burrowing Nuke

Now we understand that there is little to fear from a potential terrorist nuclear strike because their only viable source for nuclear weapons is the old Soviet stockpile, and these weapons are old, the tritium probably has leaked away long ago, and they are highly vulnerable to transportation damage, resulting in their probably not detonating.

There is, however, one kind of nuclear weapon that can withstand significant physical shock and still detonate: the burrowing nuke. It has a strong potential role to play in our fight against terrorists and the regimes that support them.

In the 1960s, the United States developed a thermonuclear device called the B61, a bomber-delivered nuke. This weapon had two interesting characteristics. It had a variable yield that could be adjusted before dropping, so that it could be tailored to a particular situation, and it had an adjustable delay that gave the delivering bomber time to retreat to a safe distance before detonation.

Over the years, the B61 went through several revisions. In August 1997, version 11 entered the U.S. nuclear arsenal. B61-11 had a significant additional characteristic: its case was hardened and its internal mechanisms were beefed up so that it could withstand a significant impact jolt. It is dropped from a great height so that it hits the ground at terminal velocity, and can penetrate up to 300 feet into compacted soil and rock.

The burrowing nuke was a reality.

Currently, the United States is continuing development of the B61, and is also working on a modification of the B83, an eighteen-inch-thick, twelve-foot-long, variable-yield, delayed-detonation nuke originally developed for the B-1 bomber force.

There is no evidence that the Soviets developed a parallel burrowing bomb of their own, so there is little danger that terrorists will get one of these devices in their hands.

These developments have gone almost unnoticed on the world stage. Current nuclear treaties allow for modification of existing warheads but prohibit developing new ones. Technically, both of these devices are modifications of earlier designs. This classification has been vigorously protested by the anti-nuclear left, particularly the Tri-Valley Communities Against a Radioactive Environment and the Federation of American Scientists, with able assistance from Greenpeace and the NRDC.

While these groups unequivocally oppose, with mindless determination, any development of nuclear weapons and any use of nuclear power, they do make a valid point. Early tests on underground nuclear explosions have indicated that such explosions are not normally contained. The explosion invariably blows a great crater in the ground, simultaneously spewing a significant amount of dirt into the air. At least in the earlier tests, this material was radioactive. The opposing groups contend that using these devices would inevitably cause significant civilian casualties.

They also maintain that penetration tests using non-explosive devices have demonstrated the limited ability of such devices to penetrate to genuinely useful levels. According to these opposing groups, typical penetrations into rock have been several dozen feet.

As is usual with these groups, their spokespeople inevitably distort the data they receive from freedom-of-information sources and occasional individuals from within the nuclear establishment.

Dr. Robert W. Nelson, from the Federation of American Scientists, is typical of these people. His bona fides include his position as a research physicist at Princeton University, but the simple fact is that he spends his time "consulting" to the Federation of American Scientists and in other anti-nuclear agitation. His "credentials" lend him credibility when he writes and appears before groups. Even the name, the Federation of American Scientists, sounds official and important. In fact, this group consists of a small number of radical anti-nuclear professional scientists and a large number of anti-nuclear attorneys and lay people.

Unlike genuine scientists and honest political opposition groups, the anti-nuclear left always uses deception and misrepresentation to put its point across, probably because in the harsh light of reality, most of its arguments fall apart.

The manner in which Nelson and the others depict the action of the burrowing nuke is to display those test results that fall on one end of the spectrum. Some tests have demonstrated a disappointing depth of penetration. If a burrowing nuke were to explode at only several feet below the surface, of course the results would be dramatically different from what is desired.

Actual drop tests, however, confirm that the device functions very well and typically penetrates 200 to 300 feet. So long as the yield of the device is sufficiently low, these explosions will produce very little surrounding damage. Furthermore, ongoing tests are developing a rocket-boost capability that will significantly enhance penetration.

A new approach is also in development. Our guided bomb capability gives us the ability to deliver several small conventional bombs sequentially into the same hole. Each successive bomb burrows deeper, so that the final bomb in the sequence, the burrowing nuke, can detonate well below 1,000 feet.

Developing this capability is fairly trivial, since all the technology is "off the shelf," in terms of current weapon capabilities. All this development really requires is modification of currently existing smart bombs so they can penetrate before exploding. The only additional development is sequencing the explosions.

The other major objection of the opponents is the collateral contamination they suspect will result from employing such devices. Their projections, once again, result from applying the worst-case scenario without consideration for current developments in low-residual-radioactivity devices.

Modern nuclear bombs normally do not produce anywhere near the level of contamination resulting from the thermonuclear behemoths of the 1960s. They are designed for explosive effect, not radioactive contamination. Furthermore, in a typical scenario, we would use a relatively small nuclear device in the low-kiloton range to take out, say, the bunker of a would-be Saddam Hussein, instead of using a megaton thermonuclear giant.

The burrowing nuke is an excellent option for taking out deeply buried, heavily armored enemy bunkers. I urge the U.S. government to move ahead full speed with the continuing development and deployment of these devices. We will all be safer when the Saddams and Qaddafis of the world have been completely eliminated.

The Dirty Bomb

Terrorists have yet another nuclear-related potential weapon in their arsenal. On March 18, 2002, the *Washington Post* published an article by staff writer Jo Warrick discussing the danger posed by old Soviet radiothermal generators (RTGs) possibly falling into the hands of terrorists. Warrick's thesis is that Strontium-90, which is used to power some of these RTGs, could be used in the construction of dirty bombs—conventional bombs that are wrapped in a layer of radioactive material, so when they explode, they spread a layer of radioactive contamination over a wide area.

In support of this thesis, Warrick cites information from the Institute for Energy and Environmental Research and the Federation of American Scientists. Both of these groups are left-wing, anti-nuclear organizations whose agendas include eliminating anything nuclear from modern life. In support of their anti-nuclear agenda, these guys routinely distort the nature of radioactivity and its effects. They can dupe the public with their exaggerations because the organizational names they have chosen evoke public trust. Warrick's real aim with this article was to use the public's fear of terrorists obtaining material for dirty nukes to eliminate further deployment of RTGs.

Within the context of this discussion, it will be useful to examine more closely what an RTG really is and what environmental threat it really poses.

An RTG consists of a radioactive source that produces heat that activates a thermocouple to produce electricity. Most Western RTGs employ plutonium as the radioactive source, since it produces the most concentrated heat from the smallest amount of material, and so allows for very compact RTGs. Since the amount of plutonium is far below that needed for a nuclear explosive device, the only danger is that related to contamination from the plutonium itself.

These compact devices are particularly useful as power sources in spacecraft that will be out of contact with concentrated sunlight, and to power devices in remote terrestrial locations, such as underwater sensors, navigational beacons, transponders, etc. Lead shielding makes up most of the mass of RTGs. Plutonium-powered units weigh only a few pounds and can mass even less when power requirements are very small. The typical Soviet-style RTGs, on the other hand, weigh in at one to three thousand pounds, because they have relatively high power requirements, and they are usually powered with Strontium-90. One can assume that the Soviets used the less-efficient Strontium-90 in their RTGs because they slated all their plutonium for nuclear weapons.

The total amount of nuclear material contained in a

typical RTG is insufficient to cause a contamination problem over greater than a few square yards. As is explained below, the Strontium-90-loaded Soviet RTGs are virtually useless as sources for dirty nukes. Most of the remaining RTGs are miles below the ocean surface or millions of miles away in deep space, doing what they were designed to do.

So, what is the "best" nuclear material to use in a dirty nuke? This depends on your objective. If you want to irritate your enemy for a very long time, say 75,000 to 4.5 billion years, you use a low-level, long-half-life material like Uranium-234 or 238, or Thorium-230. If you want to deny your enemy use of the contaminated territory for 1.5 million years, use Radium-226. Use a plutonium mixture to keep him out for 20,000 years or so.

On the other hand, if you want to harm a bunch of people and close off an area for about a decade, you use Cobalt-60. If you want to do some real damage to humans while regaining access to the area in a couple of weeks or so, use Iodine-131.

The problem with using Strontium-90 in a dirty bomb is that it really causes very little human damage. It gives out only beta particles (high-speed electrons), which we have learned can be stopped by a few feet of air, a sheet of paper, or even your skin. External burns resulting from intimate contact with concentrated Strontium-90 are indistinguishable from any other burns and heal in the same way. The only significant danger from Strontium-90 is when it is ingested and taken up in the bones, where it affects the bone marrow and can eventually cause one of several cancers. Fortunately, the body throws off any strontium relatively quickly, so even when it is ingested, the danger eventually goes away. It does hang around for thirty or so years in the environment, but you can live with it. As bomb stuff, it's really not worth the effort.

The point is, if you go to the lengths necessary to detonate a dirty bomb over one of our major cities in the United States today, you're *not* going to use Strontium-90. You're wasting your time.

Either you go for maximum short-term human impact, or you hang up a long-term keep-out sign. But you don't piddle around with strontium.

Warrick and the *Post* are nothing more than mouthpieces for the anti-nuclear left. Unfortunately, their scare tactics work, because the general public understands only what it reads and hears, and these guys supply most of the words and sounds.

CHAPTER 10

If Not Nukes, Then What?

Since it appears that nuclear weapons are not a very likely choice for terrorists, what else can they use against us? Chemical and biological weapons are two obvious choices for terrorist strikes. A small group with limited resources has essentially zero chance of obtaining a SADM, but most such groups can set up and operate a modest nerve agent manufacturing facility. A nerve agent can be released in a subway, large building, or concert hall, with devastating effects.

Chemical Weapons

Chemical weapons fall into four general categories: choking agents, blistering agents, blood agents, and organophosphate nerve agents.

Choking agents, which were extensively employed during World War I, are gasses like chlorine and phosgene. In today's world, these agents really are no alternative to the nerve agents discussed below. In order to be effective, they can only be used in an enclosed space, and it takes a very large amount of the gas to be anything other than annoying.

Similarly, blistering agents, like mustard gas, which was a frequent World War I weapon, do not have a meaningful place in today's world. The one exception would be a circumstance where a terrorist organization wanted to tie up as much of an area's medical facilities as possible but without any widespread lethal results. The consequences of a blister-gas attack are painful and very disruptive but not usually fatal.

Most blood agents are based on cyanide and can be used in lethal amounts. Since lethal cyanide blood levels are similar to lethal levels of phosgene, there really is little difference between blood agents and lethal choking gases. Both require enclosed spaces to be effective, and neither is as effective as nerve agents.

Organophosphates originally were developed as insecticides. In the early part of the twentieth century, there was even limited production and use of early versions of what are now called nerve agents—before their lethal effect on animals was fully understood. Currently, four substances occupy the nerve-agent platform. Their ease of manufacture, their volatility, and their lethality all affect which of these is more suited to terrorist activities.

VX nerve agent is very lethal. Six to ten milligrams of this substance absorbed through the skin or ten milligrams breathed into the lungs as an aerosol will kill. For reference, a grain of rice weighs about ten milligrams. VX is stable; it sticks to things as a slightly sticky, oily film. Its high toxicity and ability to remain on surfaces for a long time make this agent an excellent killing weapon. Fortunately, it is very difficult to manufacture, so VX is unlikely to appear as the next terrorist weapon of choice.

A Soman nerve agent dose is three to five times the size of a lethal VX dose. Soman is more volatile than VX, so it dissipates more quickly; but its main use still is to coat surfaces rather than as a gas. Furthermore, it is just as difficult to manufacture as VX, so given a choice between Soman and VX, a terrorist will probably choose VX.

Both Sarin and Tabun are considerably less lethal, requiring about fifteen times the breathing dose and

200 times the skin dose of VX to be lethal. Sarin is very volatile, so that it is most effective as a gas. This makes it excellent for use in enclosed areas like a large building or a subway. Because of restricted access to intermediate substances required in its manufacture, however, it is difficult to make. Tabun, the oldest nerve agent, while more volatile than VX and Soman, is significantly less volatile than Sarin, and it is very easy to manufacture. It is probable, therefore, that most terrorist nerve-gas SIS operations will use Tabun.

Following World War II, the Allies seized over twelve thousand tons of Tabun. Much of this was subsequently destroyed, but there may still be large quantities stashed in some forgotten warehouse. Given the worldwide presence of terrorist groups such as al Qaeda, it is distinctly possible that World War II vintage Tabun nerve agent forms a significant part of the arsenals of these organizations.

Biological Weapons

On a scale of cost for the number of civilian casualties accomplished, nothing holds a candle to biological agents. Conventional weapons will cost approximately $2,000 per square kilometer of civilian casualties for a large-scale operation against a civilian population. The same damage over the same area using nuclear weapons will cost less than half—$800. Using nerve agents reduces the cost to $600. But if you apply biological weapons, the cost is a paltry $1.

What is an effective biological agent? In the aftermath of the New York World Trade Center attack, the United States experienced a series of anthrax incidents. As of this writing, their source remains unknown. What is known, however, is that handling anthrax is not particularly difficult. It is not contagious, so infection requires direct contact with the spores. Furthermore, most infections are of the skin variety, which—while annoying—are not fatal. Even the inhaled type is completely reversible if it is treated right away, and anthrax is responsive to a variety of antibiotics. Its singular advantage is that it is easy to manufacture. Anthrax, therefore, can be effective in tying up medical facilities and generating widespread panic and disruption, but it is not very effective as a lethal biological agent.

Smallpox is another frequently mentioned biological agent. Smallpox is deadly, it is very contagious in the pox stage, and the only real treatment is inoculation either before or within three or four days after infection. Fortunately, despite these facts, smallpox is not really an effective biological agent for two simple reasons. The first is that there are only two known supplies of the virus, in the United States and in Russia. We know where both are located, where they are kept under maximum security. There is very little chance that any more exists. The second reason is that the infectious phase of the illness is also the phase where the victim is seriously stressed by the virus. A patient flat on his or her back is unlikely to infect other people.

Botulism is the organism responsible for food poisoning. It certainly can be spread by infecting food across the country at supermarkets and in buffets, but even more than anthrax, botulism is rarely deadly, and less likely to cause panic.

Ricin is a very toxic white powder extracted from castor beans. While it certainly is dangerous when ingested, it is not a very practical weapon. In London in 1978, the Bulgarian dissident Georgi Markow was killed when injected with this poison from the tip of an umbrella while he was waiting for a bus. One on one, ricin is an effective biological weapon, but it is not useful for spreading mass terror.

Bubonic plague killed millions in past centuries. Its effectiveness, however, was in large measure the result of unclean lifestyle habits. It is very unlikely that this plague would propagate far in modern America.

Tularemia is similar to anthrax in nearly every respect, including its symptoms and treatment. And like anthrax, while it can instill panic and disruption, it will not be very effective as a weapon.

Ebola hemorrhagic fever can kill in just a few hours. It is highly contagious. There is no known cure and no prophylactic vaccination. In the hands of a very sophisticated enemy, Ebola can be a highly effective biological weapon. The need for sophistication arises from the extreme difficulty involved in maintaining the viability of the Ebola virus. It takes the infrastructure of a major biochemical laboratory to manufacture and transport viable Ebola. This generally is beyond the capability of a terrorist organization.

There is one other way to infect a target nation with Ebola. Assemble a sufficiently large number of simians so that you can sustain a loss of six or seven creatures daily. Isolate a simian infected with Ebola, keeping in mind that it will die within three to four hours. Before the infected animal dies, pass the infection to the next creature, and so on, while transporting the entire batch to the target country. With a bit of luck, you should be able to pass the infection directly into the population. Once the infection gains a foothold, only the most draconian measures will bring it to a halt. Considering the logistics for pulling something like this off, however, it is very unlikely that an unsophisticated terrorist organization will be able to use Ebola hemorrhagic fever as an effective biological weapon.

That pretty much covers the field. While any disease can potentially be used as a weapon, realistically, anthrax and tularemia can cause significant panic and disruption, but only Ebola will cause any widespread casualties. Since Ebola requires greater sophistication than normally available to typical terrorists, biological attacks do not pose a meaningful threat.

Manpad Weapons

We have examined some of the weapon options available to terrorists like al Qaeda. Recently, another grim possibility has come to light.

On November 17, 1995, at 10:20 P.M., Lufthansa Flight 405 and British Airways Flight 226 were flying thirty to forty miles apart on parallel paths towards Europe, having just taken off from Kennedy International Airport. Suddenly, an object moving in the opposite direction passed 2,000 to 3,000 feet to the left and above the British Airways plane, and shortly thereafter it passed the Lufthansa plane.

Both pilots reported that the object looked like a missile, with a bright nose and a long green tail with white "smoke." Air-traffic control at Boston could not find the object on its tracking radar.

On June 26, 1996, at 10:29 P.M., TWA Flight 848 bound for Rome from Kennedy passed eleven nautical miles south of Shinnecock Inlet on Long Island. At the same time, the U.S. Coast Guard received multiple reports of three bright flares launched into the sky twenty-five nautical miles south of Shinnecock Inlet. The pilot of the aircraft apparently did not see these "flares."

On July 17, 1996, at 9:45 P.M., TWA Flight 800 went down shortly after taking off from Kennedy. Many witnesses testified that they had seen what appeared to be one or two missiles strike the aircraft just before it blew up in the sky.

On November 16, 1996, at 9:25 P.M., on its way from Kennedy to Frankfurt, Pakistan International Airlines

Flight 712 reported "some kind of large firecracker rocket" rising from below the aircraft, passing from left to right across its path. This object was seen on radar at the Boston air-traffic control site. The pilot of TWA Flight 884 bound for Tel Aviv and following close behind Pakistan International 712 commented ironically by radio that firecrackers don't go past 16,000 feet. His plane was immediately diverted.

On December 12, 1996, Saudi Arabian Airlines Flight 35 inbound to Kennedy observed a bright green object pass from right to left across its path.

On August 9, 1997, at 6:07 P.M., Swissair Flight 127 bound for Zurich from Kennedy nearly collided with a bright airborne object moving at high speed in the opposite direction.

On July 16, 1999, John F. Kennedy, Jr., was killed in a mysterious small-plane crash in the same general area as these other incidents.

On November 12, 2001, at 9:17 A.M., American Airlines Flight 587 crashed shortly after takeoff from Kennedy, bound for Santo Domingo. Officially, the vertical stabilizer failed catastrophically and fell off.

These eight incidents are but a small sampling of events around the world that may have a common thread. They all could have been caused by one of several small missiles that have proliferated in the world of black-market weapon sales ever since the United States introduced the Stinger missile to the Afghani Mujahideen in the late 1980s.

Their generic name is Manpad weapons, short for Man-Portable Air Defense. For the fierce Afghan fighters, the Stinger made victory possible against the otherwise unassailable Soviet helicopters. It changed the face of the war in Afghanistan.

Since the war against the Soviets in Afghanistan ended, hundreds of Stingers have not been accounted for. Furthermore, the Red Chinese stole the Stinger plans and now manufacture thousands of similar missiles each year, selling them to the highest bidder.

The Soviet arsenal also contained a small Manpad that, although not quite as small and reliable as the Stinger, could find devastating use in a terrorist's hands. The Czechs designed and manufactured a similar unit; it has found its way into terrorist arsenals as well.

The precursor to the Stinger was the Redeye—bigger, slower, more cumbersome, not as smart—and not all of these are accounted for either.

A Stinger missile, or similar Manpad, is deadly to passenger airliners as they take off or land. They are small, lightweight, and can easily be hidden in a car. Heat sensors and small computers guide them straight to an airliner's engines—assuming they retain their correct alignment. Their ceiling is about 12,000 feet at about Mach 2.0, or twice the speed of sound. An airliner has no chance when a Stinger missile is aimed at it.

The pilot would not even see the missile coming and would only react when it hit the engine or an area nearby. The tip of the Stinger can be equipped with various types of explosives, but just the impact of the missile is enough to bring down a plane. The pilot will hear a thud when the missile hits, and people on the ground will hear the same thing and observe a small fireball at the impact point.

I am not necessarily suggesting that all eight incidents presented earlier were Manpad events, but I am suggesting that they could have been. It is likely that black-market Stingers have undergone relatively severe transportation shock and misalignment. This could cause such a missile to miss its intended target, which would explain why most of the incidents related above appear to be misses.

If one makes the assumption that one or more of these incidents was a malfunctioning Manpad launched by a terrorist controlled by al Qaeda, then one can logically conclude that al Qaeda probably is in the market for Manpads that hit their targets—new and undamaged, to be certain.

On November 6, 2002, Hong Kong authorities arrested three men who were attempting to purchase four Stinger missiles from undercover FBI agents. In payment, they were offering a half-ton of heroin and five tons of hashish. This is not speculation—it's a cold, hard fact. Had the source for these Manpads been anything other than undercover good guys, it is a near certainty that four airliners would have been brought down in the following weeks or months.

Two of the arrested men were Pakistani, but one was an American citizen of Indian extraction. According to statements these men made to arresting authorities, the Stingers were intended for al Qaeda, although the men claimed to be acting as agents for the purchase.

The astonishing amount of heroin and hashish they were prepared to trade for the Stingers is a measure of just how badly al Qaeda wants Manpad missiles in good working order. Al Qaeda cell members clearly are not rocket scientists, or we would have seen many more downed civilian airliners. They appear, however, to have unlimited access to narcotics.

Thwarted in its efforts to convert money in banks to weapons, al Qaeda has apparently turned to the well-established worldwide drug-distribution network to gain access to weapons, ammunition, and possibly chemical and biological agents. It is humanly impossible to prevent every transaction from happening, and all it takes is for a few drugs-for-weapons deals to close for al Qaeda to spread another form of terror around the world.

Because of the innocuous appearance and easy concealability of Stingers and other Manpads, no flight anywhere is immune from this threat. According to Michael Ruppert in *From the Wilderness Publications,*

a reliable source long connected with intelligence operations, as many as thirty-five Soviet-made Manpads
were smuggled into the United States from Canada in
late 2001. It's only a matter of time before one of these,
or a Stinger purchased with drugs on the worldwide
black market, brings down a passenger liner in a way
that leaves no doubt as to what happened.

That scenario appeared closer to playing out on
August 12, 2003, when FBI agents arrested British
national Hemant Lakhani in New Jersey and two others in Manhattan who were involved in a plot to import
and sell a Russian Manpad to terrorists.

There is little that can be done about these threats
except to nip them in the bud, which is exactly what
our guys did. Working in close cooperation with British
and Russian officials over several months, the FBI
finally arrested Lakhani, an unlicensed British arms
dealer, when he attempted to sell a Russian SA-18 Igla
Manpad to an undercover FBI agent posing as a
Muslim terrorist.

There is more to this story, however. It appears that
Lakhani did not actually develop his Russian contacts
on his own but had significant help from Russian
undercover agents. In fact, the Manpad he procured
for resale to the American "Muslim" was not an actual
working missile but a realistic training mockup supplied by those undercover agents.

ABC News revealed shortly thereafter that the government's key witness in this case was an informant
seeking leniency on federal drug charges. Furthermore,
Lakhani may not have carried out this operation on his
own. He appears to have been a small-time operator with
a bark more vicious than his bite—until his attitude
brought him to the attention of British authorities, who
contacted the Americans, who, with the Russians, set
Lakhani up for his fall.

So the question here is, do we score one for the good

guys, or do we chalk this one up to our guys trying too hard?

I don't have a problem with locking Lakhani away for his natural life. Regardless of the circumstances, he really did believe he was arranging for a Manpad to shoot down a large American plane. But while our guys were playing cat-and-mouse games with this small-timer, how many real missile sales into the United States went undetected?

Airline Missile Defense

This brings us back to the main issue. What can we do to prevent the inevitable, besides intercepting potential Manpad shipments?

Quite a lot, it turns out. There are viable missile-defense systems that can be installed on civilian airliners.

Defense contractors in both the U.S. and Israel have been working on the problem ever since it was first identified. Their efforts have produced two approaches to the solution. Both use radar onboard the aircraft to detect incoming missiles. Since all Manpads rely upon some kind of heat-seeking technology, one defensive system automatically launches hot flares to divert the missiles from the plane's jet engines, which they would otherwise track. The other concept illuminates the incoming missiles with intense laser beams that confuse their guidance systems.

Both systems have been manufactured in Israel and the United States and have been extensively tested on military and civilian aircraft. The systems appear to work very well, with virtually a 100 percent kill rate against known Manpad types, even the more sophisticated Igla and Stinger systems that include a proximity fuse and complex electronics to overcome jamming attempts.

The flare systems are inherently less expensive than the laser systems, but they introduce an added hazard to civilian aircraft because of their combustibility. The laser systems weigh just over three hundred pounds and operate with full autonomy, informing the pilot in real time that a missile is being diverted. The laser system can be retrofitted on any civilian aircraft during a short downtime—twenty-four hours.

This is the good news.

The bad news is that current production models cost over $3 million apiece. There is a ready solution for this, however.

In full production, these same laser units will cost only $1.2 million, installed. The U.S. civilian air fleet consists of 6,800 planes of varying sizes. For the sake of this exercise, let's assume that the average plane can carry 250 passengers.

The initial cost for manufacture and installation of this system on all our civilian passenger aircraft amounts to $8.2 billion. I suggest that Congress pick up this tab, as a "loan" to the airline firms. Then, each passenger will be charged a $25 surcharge to repay this money. The cost would be recovered in 326.4 million passenger flights, which calculates out to 1.3 million airline trips, or just under 200 flights per plane. This means that the airline industry could fully repay the taxpayers this onetime cost in about a year.

Even though we have intercepted at least one attempt to sell Manpads to terrorists in the United States, without a viable antimissile defense, the inevitable will happen: a planeload of innocent Americans will be blasted out of the air. We can install systems on all our passenger aircraft that will virtually guarantee that this will not happen.

If Congress chooses, we can accomplish the installation of these laser systems on all 6,800 of our civilian aircraft within a week or so after the defenses are built (give contractors a month to build all 6,800) and pay it off over the following year at a cost of $25 per passenger, per flight.

In my book that's a bargain.

The Cold War is behind us. Nevertheless, we need a strong military and weapons that deter. The real threat today, however, is the SIS. We need to retain all our options, including nuclear, to combat this threat. We must be prepared to defend ourselves against the nerve agents Sarin and Tabun, and our general population should be educated regarding the limited threat posed by anthrax and tularemia.

The bottom line is that a free nation willing to defend itself decisively will maintain a viable presence in the world long after terrorist opposition has been relegated to a historical footnote.

CHAPTER 11

Morality and Ethics, or "It's Not My Fault!"

Have you had something stolen from you lately? Do you know somebody who has? Aside from the terrorism threat, do you believe the world is less safe today than it was twenty years ago? Have you asked yourself why societal values seem to be changing for the worse?

Pick up any newspaper; listen to any newscast. Visit a courtroom; watch C-Span. Even if you don't have a standard against which you can measure what you see and hear, you will be left with the impression that there is something fundamentally wrong with today's society, September 11 notwithstanding.

You are not alone. Across the civilized world, men and women publicly debate the underlying reasons for this singular turn of events. More often than any other, the issue of morality is raised, with the usual conclusion being that Western civilization has turned away from God and the precepts that underlie Judeo-Christian thought.

Occasionally, someone will point out that similar problems are developing in societies that do not subscribe to traditional Western religious philosophy. Depending on the speaker's own perspective, the answer usually turns on a "lack of Christian values" within these other societies (which begs the question), or sage observations on how in these societies—as in ours—morals are being ignored as these societies turn away from their religious roots. As cases in point, they cite Mormon communities or even strict Islamic societies, where crime is nearly unknown.

Common to all these "insights" is the unchallenged assumption that religious principle underlies morality, and as a society turns from traditional religious roots, it loses touch with its moral roots as well.

Ironically, within our own society, those who reject traditional religious values (for whatever reason—scientific, philosophical, etc.) tend to embrace "esoteric" alternatives to fill the void and supply a moral tone or framework for their lives. Witness the resurgence of astrology, crystalology, pyramidology, Scientology, and the many other pseudoscientific worldviews on one hand, and general interest in Buddhism, Zoroastrianism, B'hai, and other "foreign" religious philosophies on the other. Even within the framework of traditional Judeo-Christian thought, denominations have arisen that attempt to integrate morality and religious thought on some "higher" level.

The Basis for Morality

This idea is pervasive: morality results from and is guided by religion. But is this really true? Back in 1947, Phillip Wylie, the popular cultural gadfly, wrote *An Essay on Morals,* a slender volume wherein he attempted to address this issue. More than anything else, this work is a discussion of Carl Jung's concept of archetypal figures and the collective race memory that forms a significant part of Jung's writings. After his first edition reached reviewers, Wylie found himself panned by critics. The common theme of their rebukes was that Wylie had not a clue about Jung's perspective. Religious leaders were outraged, and the intellectual community followed the critics in their knowing putdowns of Wylie. (In his inimitable way, Wylie had managed to step on everybody's toes once more.)

While all this was going on, Carl Jung wrote to

Wylie, stating that he found Wylie's approach to his work "well chosen." As might be expected, Wylie took full advantage of Jung's letter in the introduction to the 1951 second edition of *An Essay on Morals.*

According to Wylie (and fully endorsed by Jung), there is nothing at all mystical about the apparent human collective subconscious mind or memory. We are the current end product of one of Nature's evolutionary paths. As we trace back along our evolutionary branch, we discover more and more common elements with members of other species.

One very large difference stands out, however. Human cognitive ability far exceeds that of any other species on this planet. Even when we consider such interesting phenomena as the female gorilla Mitzi, who learned several dozen words in sign language, there still is a vast gap between our ability to think, imagine, ponder, and so forth and that of any other species. And yet we share a large common pool of genetic material with other species, including much that has been determined to control instinct in these other species.

Why, then, do humans not exhibit the same kinds of instinctual patterns that control all other animals? We do, Wylie says, but because we have this incredible ability to think, we ask, "Why?" The complexity of our thinking patterns, however, causes this "why?" to be buried in our subconscious minds, where it inevitably seeks and ultimately finds answers. These answers take the form of mental constructs that appear universally across all human societies, throughout all human history. Jung calls them *archetypes,* and he successfully mapped these universal images to specific instinctual patterns he observed in animals.

Jung's mapping is not universally accepted, but his underlying insight is powerful. Once we understand that all religions, all "moral philosophies," all ideologies have the common basis of human instinct gene patterns, we can more clearly understand why, when religious faith declines, another "faith" must take its place. Inevitably, upon close examination, the similarities between this new "faith" and the old will completely overshadow their superficial differences.

Take, for example, the Soviet Communist party, which by Stalin's rule had effectively replaced the Russian Orthodox Church as the state religion. Here is a partial comparison between the archetypal representations from the Russian Orthodox Church and the Soviet Communist party.

Russian Orthodox Church	Soviet Communist Party
Trinity	Marx, Engels, Lenin
Holy Virgin	Mother Russia
John the Baptist	Trotsky
Jesus	Stalin
Patriarch	Communist party chairman
Holy Bible	Das Kapital

We will accept as a premise, therefore, that we are bound by patterns of instinct. These patterns manifest themselves as archetypal figures haunting our subconscious minds with sufficient sameness that the ghosts and gods and goblins we create—no matter where or when—are more alike than not. Is it possible, under these circumstances, to formulate a moral philosophy that remains independent of these driving archetypes?

Enter ethics.

Ethics

There always has been confusion surrounding the two concepts, morality and ethics. Before we look closer, however, let us set aside any semantic problems.

I once witnessed a conversation among several women regarding the color of a piece of cloth. The color was subtle—not your basic red, black, blue, green, or yellow. Picking out a name for this color could have been an interesting exercise in advertising psychology. In this case, however, each of the women could clearly see the color; whatever name somebody somewhere might have assigned to it had absolutely no bearing on what it actually was. Nevertheless, these ladies spent fifteen minutes or so arguing among themselves about the color's name. I suspect they thought they were discussing the color, but to me, the uninvolved observer, it was clear that their discussion was about what to call the color. From my engineering point of view, all they really needed to do was agree on any name—fratuti, for example—and then use that name for the color. No matter what they called it, the color would remain exactly what it was. These women had been waylaid by the semantics of their problem so that they completely missed the real point of their discussion: what should they name the color.

A similar situation frequently happens when we deal with the concepts of morality and ethics. Generally in America today we use the words "morality" and "ethics" interchangeably. We get wrapped up in giving two names to what we perceive as one concept, and then we argue about those names. Actually, these are two concepts having two names. If we define our terms beforehand, we should have little difficulty in distinguishing between them. With this in mind, I will, therefore, define morality as religion derived and ethics as derived from first principles. The difference, then, is not a function of what, but rather of how derived. Ethical behavior (derived from first principles) can be moral within this context if it also can be derived from religious principle. Ethical behavior can be immoral within this context, if religion condemns it;

and, of course, it can also be amoral if religion does not address it. Likewise, moral behavior can be ethical or unethical; and it can also be non-ethical, in the sense that it falls outside the purview of ethics.

The problem in society today is that organized religion, which has dictated moral behavior, is losing favor with the general population. Since neither our families nor our schools are teaching anything resembling ethics, the only available replacements are the "esoteric" alternatives that are becoming so pervasive or the more visceral "street rules" that govern urban gangs. The result is predictable.

Is there a genuine basis for ethics outside of the moral religious strictures that seem to bind our society? Can we really start with first principle and derive an ethical framework that will work today, that can form the basis for reasonable social interaction, that can be taught in our schools and form an essential part of family life?

For simplicity, isolate one human on an island, and let him create what he needs for survival. (During this analogy, we will ignore the requirements for physical survival, other than to stipulate their background necessity and availability.) By himself, this solitary human requires no theoretical constructs—no ethics. He does whatever he wishes, however he wishes, whenever he wishes.

Now double the population of the island.

Enter ethics.

The simple fact of adding another human immediately creates the need for interaction, no matter how rare; and interaction mandates rules of behavior. No matter how informal or unstructured, in the final analysis, the presence of more than one individual mandates some kind of interactive relationship, a set of rules, ethics.

Realistically, what are these rules? One can successfully argue that there are a large number of ways two or more individuals can work out their interrelationships. While this is true, there remain several fundamental elements that are common to all of them.

For example, if a society allows wanton killing of humans in the thoughtless manner in which a person steps on a bug, it is easy to show that this society will internally destruct. Similarly, one can review the rules of our current society and determine other rules that are absolutely necessary for the survival of society.

As society grows, the number and complexity of these necessary rules also grow, until a more general state is reached where the population has stabilized, and the set of rules—the ethics framework—has achieved stasis. There are sufficient rules to govern nearly any contingency, including "contingent" rules that address the odd exception. If one then formalizes these rules, so that they can be stated logically along with their obvious derivative paths, then one has a formal ethics system that can be taught in class to young members of society, and imposed on the impressionable minds of children in the home.

The result is a society with a common set of ethical underpinnings, rules of behavior that do not depend on religious training or perspective, a framework that will not dissipate in the face of changing belief systems. This goal is realistically achievable if educators throughout the society are specifically charged with its implementation. The difficulty lies not in creating the concept, structuring the class material, or disseminating the knowledge, but simply in convincing the educators—the teachers—that it must happen. Within limits, legislation can help, but in the final analysis, a thoroughly convinced teacher in every classroom will make it happen.

Individual Freedom

America today is a statist bureaucracy that gives passing lip service to individual liberty but actually exercises more control over individual lives in more ways than ever in its history. American society exercises this control at every level: from the kind of necktie an attorney may wear before the Supreme Court to the admission standards at a community college; from what a publisher may print in a magazine to what one calls a person whose eyes do not work; from what parts of a body must remain concealed (on a body that is one of only two models in a multibillion population) to an "acceptable" name for Sambo's restaurant chain.

An underlying American principle is supremacy of the individual. Our founding fathers seemed to say that control of everything rests with the individual except where it is clearly impossible for the individual to exercise such control. Only then does government take control, but always that government closest to the problem—local and regional government first, then state, and finally national, and then only for matters that go beyond the interests of individual states.

Our founders proclaimed these principles when they declared their independence, and they embodied them in the Constitution, which they created to guide the federal system that would control their lives, and their children's lives, and their children's children's. . . . Obviously, they did a good job, because the Constitution is the oldest still-used constitutional document in all the history of our planet. They built in sufficient flexibility to maintain its currency and sufficient backbone to keep it viable.

The American federal system that they created can be summarized in this brief outline.

1. Powers of the national government. The Constitution delegates to the national government certain expressly

enumerated executive, legislative, and judicial powers, certain implied powers that may be reasonably inferred from the express powers, and certain inherent powers that derive from the very nature of a national government.

2. Powers of the states. The Constitution reserves to the states all powers not expressly granted to the national government nor specifically denied to the states.

3. National supremacy. The Constitution holds the national government to be supreme in those limited areas in which it operates.

4. Constitutional limits. The Constitution imposes restraints on both national and state governments to preserve the federal system and to preserve individual freedom.

Diverging interpretations of the American federal system clashed even before it went into effect. With the passing of time, these differing views have evolved, but the fundamental difference between them is as real today as it was back then.

Thomas Jefferson insisted on reserving to the individual or to the lowest possible government unit anything not specifically reserved by the Constitution to a higher unit. On a more practical level, Jefferson saw the Constitution as an intergovernmental compact created by the citizens of the several states through their state representatives. As such, the real power rested with the states. That was the power the people controlled. The federal government was tasked only with those things beyond the scope of the individual states.

Alexander Hamilton, on the other hand, argued that the federal government, in order to carry out its mandate, needed to acquire many powers not specifically granted it by the Constitution. Hamilton rejected Jefferson's intergovernmental compact in favor of a concept that bypassed state governments and looked directly to the people for constitutional authority. In effect, Hamilton moved the power to regulate individuals' lives from the "local" to the "federal" level. When the dust settled, Chief Justice John Marshall summarized in McCulloch v. Maryland: "Let the end be legitimate, let it be within the scope of the Constitution, and all means which are appropriate, which are plainly adapted to that end, which are not prohibited, but consistent with the letter and spirit of the Constitution, are constitutional."

Jefferson had lost, and therein lay the seeds of a problem that still affects us today.

Clearly, neither Jefferson nor Hamilton could foresee today's instant-communication networks. Neither of them could have predicted C-Span's ability to eavesdrop on the daily activities of our national legislators. Ironically, I suspect each would have seen these developments as supporting his own argument. Hamilton would have correctly pointed out that such capabilities give directly to the people the power to control their national legislators. Jefferson certainly would argue, however, that the ability to control two senators and one representative does not give you control over your life, whereas the ability to monitor closely the activities of local and state legislators just may make such control possible.

This, then, is the crux of the matter. Given that some level of regulation over individual lives is necessary, who is better able to conduct this regulation? Is it a national legislature composed of members from fifty different states and several territories, concerned with national matters, dealing with national priorities? Is it a state legislature that focuses strictly on the needs and concerns of a much smaller geographic and political entity? Or is it local county or city government?

Who defines "legitimate" and "appropriate"? All "those" guys, or "our" guys? Many state legislatures have enacted motorcycle helmet laws. Clearly, the majority of legislators believed it was "legitimate" and "appropriate" for bikers to be helmeted. They invoked statistics about lower injury rates for helmet wearers. They calculated higher costs to society for supplying care to injured helmetless bikers without adequate insurance. Counter-arguments about an individual's right to make responsible choices (or not), about usurping rights not specifically granted to government, fell on deaf ears. Arguments for enforcing specific financial requirements on bikers to offset society's cost for their potential injuries went unheeded.

This was "our" guys who did this, state-level politicians focused on state interests. This has happened across America in nearly every state. Who defines "legitimate" and "appropriate"?

Jefferson would answer: you, whenever possible. And when you can't, then the government closest to you, over which you have the greatest control.

Hamilton would answer: the federal government, whenever possible. And when it cannot because of jurisdictional restrictions or for other reasons, then the government closest to it.

Mandatory seatbelt laws are another example of this thinking. Government assumes a responsibility not specifically granted to it, thereby removing from the individual the responsibility for making another self-preserving, rational decision. Clearly, the Hamiltonian point of view prevails today. The answer to "who defines 'legitimate' and 'appropriate'?" rarely is you, and frequently is the Feds. And when it isn't the Feds, it is "our guys" at the highest possible state level.

This approach leads to increasing amounts of unnecessary regulation and control, regulation and control that individuals would never condone on a personal level but that they accept with helpless resignation because it is imposed on them from above. Arguments about saving lives, making people safer, and protecting our environment simply do not wash. Our Constitution is not about saving lives, making people safer, or protecting our environment; it's about personal freedom, period.

Prove that my driving fifty-five miles per hour makes you safer on the highway, and you have my attention. Prove that it makes me safer and base a speed limit on this, and you've taken from me a choice I should be making. Hold me legally accountable for the consequences of my reckless driving and enforce this, and you'll keep my attention. Fine me when you catch me speeding, and I'll buy a radar detector.

We are losing sight of a fundamental principle. In a society of free individuals, we each must act in our own rational self-interest. We each are fully accountable for our actions. Society must enforce this fact, must ensure that each individual never escapes the consequences of irresponsible behavior.

It isn't a question of whether or not a result is beneficial. It is not even a question of right or wrong. It is a question of responsibility, accountability, and culpability.

Constitutional government is about protecting you from me and me from you and protecting us from them. That's it: no Great Society, no national health plan, no golden parachute. . . . To paraphrase Marshall's famous summary in McCulloch v. Maryland, let these (protecting you from me and me from you and us from them) be the only legitimate scope of the Constitution, and all means which are appropriate, which are plainly adapted to that end, which are not prohibited, but consistent with the letter and spirit of the Constitution, are constitutional.

Or put another way, let the Constitution be the instrument that enforces the spirit behind the American Indian name for a well-known Michigan lake: Argogagogmanchuagagogchaubunaugungamog, which loosely translated into English means: you fish on your side; I'll fish on my side; and we'll both stay away from the middle.

Victocrats Rule

Another element in modern society is the "victim complex," where we tend to blame everything but the actual cause for many problems: addiction, alcoholism, gun violence, etc.

One of the most significant apparent differences between primitive and modern societies is how each perceives reality. Without an understanding of the real causes and effects within nature, primitive man created his own. He animated his world. Objects assumed purpose, good or evil intentions. Since his own society quite obviously thrived within a structure, primitive man created an analogous structure for his animated world.

Today we know a great deal about the causes and effects surrounding us. Our insights into weather, for instance, have caused us to abandon the rain dance in favor of more effective prediction and control methods (although some would argue that there is little difference in the outcome).

The ancients were not entirely clear on the relationship between responsibility and accountability either. When a rain dance failed to produce rain, did this result from the rain god's anger—his fickle attitude— or was it simply a result of ineffective dancing? The rain god obviously was responsible for making rain, but who was really accountable when the rain didn't come?

Now, of course, we don't see things this way. Someday, perhaps, we will find ways to control weather patterns—to make rain—but for now we rightfully ignore responsibility and accountability in this area. On the other hand, we diligently pursue these concepts across a vast spectrum of human and non-human activity.

Unfortunately, recognizing accountability too often devolves into assigning blame. Years ago, I served under a submarine skipper who confused these concepts. When something went awry, the first thing this man did was look around for the nearest officer, whom he promptly blamed for the problem. The result was that in an emergency his officers scattered to avoid being blamed, leaving him without the expertise he needed to solve his problem. Implicit in this man's actions was his reluctance to accept his absolute accountability as the submarine commander.

In a manner that harks back to primitive perceptions, blaming (sloughing off responsibility, rejecting accountability) has become a stupefying problem within modern society. It's not the drunk's fault—he's an alcoholic. It's not the mugger's fault—he's an addict. It's not the gunman's fault—we sold him a gun. It's not the driver's fault—we let him drive too fast.

We blame alcoholism, drug addiction, guns, and speed while absolving the alcoholic, the addict, the gunman, the irresponsible driver.

Alcoholism sounds more sophisticated than Bacchus, but the ancients blamed the animated object, whereas we just blame the object. They understood that accountability rests squarely on the shoulders of someone who is accountable. In their scientific naïveté, they spread accountability well beyond the human race, yet they still attached it to beings.

What excuse do we have?

CHAPTER 12

Starlight, Star Bright: The Cosmic Speed Limit

What is a theory? I recently asked this question of a relatively learned friend. He answered by comparing theory to fact, stating that a theory was a nonsubstantive explanation for a set of facts. As more facts become known, he said, theoretical explanations give way to factual ones. Ultimately, a theory may be vindicated (proved by fact), partially vindicated (partially substantiated by fact but also partially disproved), or overturned.

In one sense my friend is right. When a historian uses this word, one can assume he gives it my friend's meaning. And when a poet uses the word. And a writer. Almost any nonscientist, in fact. On the other hand, when a scientist or engineer means what my friend defined, he uses the words "hypothesis" or "hypothetical." When he uses the words "theory" or "theoretical," however, he means something entirely different.

In scientific usage, "theoretical" is the opposite of "empirical." In measuring the speed of sound in sea water, for example, researchers frequently use an equation that consists of a long series of increasingly smaller functions of density, salinity, temperature, and pressure. This equation is the result of measuring the speed of sound in sea water under a very large number of differing situations, and then deriving the equation from these data. It is called an empirical equation.

Another approach to the same problem is to create a mathematical model of the ocean, and to derive an equation for the speed of sound that depends upon the mathematical structure of this model. This equation is called a theoretical equation.

Both equations are real. One is derived empirically, the other theoretically. Each is subject to error, and each is only as good as its ability to predict the actual speed of sound in any given situation. Ultimately, scientists attempt to replace empirical equations with theoretical ones, as they gain a deeper understanding.

Albert Einstein's theory of relativity is a set of theoretical equations derived from a mathematical model of the universe. They explain many things in our daily lives: why transistors work, for example. Quantum mechanics is another theory in physics. It explains why nuclear reactors work.

These theories are real and they predict events with great precision. They are theoretical—and they are true.

When an individual applies the historian's definition to the scientist's use of the word "theory," the result is confusion and misinformation. While the scientist distinguishes between model-derived and empirical solutions, the layperson believes he distinguishes between assumption and reality.

For the layperson, fact ultimately displaces theory. For the scientist, theory ultimately explains fact.

A case in point is the theory of biological evolution, probably one of the best established and most widely accepted scientific theories. Well-intentioned people who don't understand the meaning of the word "theory" have assumed that the *theory* of evolution is an *unproved hypothesis.* Many of these individuals object to evolution on religious grounds, and use their misunderstanding of the nature of a scientific theory to reject one of the most essential unifying concepts in biological science.

In an ideal world, a scientist collects data, and then creates a theoretical construct that explains their existence. Following this, the construct is tested by various means. Over time, the original construct typically undergoes modification as additional data become known. Occasionally a construct has to be discarded and replaced with something else, because new data cannot be fit into the old framework.

A good example of this is the old phlogiston theory, wherein a substance called phlogiston was believed to be consumed when something burned. Researchers weighed an object before burning, and then again after burning. Since it seemed to weigh less after burning, obviously, something had been consumed: phlogiston. The English clergyman Joseph Priestly discovered that when he heated mercury in a jar it became coated with a red substance. If he put a mouse into the jar after the red substance formed, the mouse died. When the red ash evaporated, a glowing splinter thrust into the jar would burst into flame, and a mouse would become hyperactive. When Priestly described his experiment to the French chemist Antoine Lavoisier, the latter immediately realized from his own experiments that Priestly had discovered a new substance, which he called oxygen. Lavoisier had determined through careful measurements that substances that burned actually took on weight. He concluded that Priestly had discovered the substance that supplied that weight: oxygen. Consequently the phlogiston theory was discarded in favor of Priestly's and Lavoisier's new theory.

Philosophical (and religious) arguments typically go the other way. You start out with a construct (hypothesis), which you then attempt to verify with data. If the construct really does reflect the outside world, then the data will tend to verify the construct. Unfortunately, when the data are at variance with the construct, ideologues typically will either ignore the data or twist and modify them so that they fit. Only very rarely do they modify the construct to fit the data.

An example of one such modification was when the Roman Catholic Church finally accepted the long-established scientific fact that the sun, and not the Earth, was the center of the solar system.

In today's world, the confusion of the difference between "theory" and "hypothesis" by nonscientific people has resulted in a schism separating fundamental Christianity from modern biological science. Simply stated, from the religious perspective, the biblical construct currently is considered more important than the data. In effect, people holding this point of view have decided that the biblical Old Testament "explanation" for how humans came to be is "absolutely" correct. Consequently, they are forced to modify their and the public's perception of the overwhelming data that supports biological evolution as scientists currently understand it.

This is so very unfortunate, because they accomplish two things: (1) they convince honest people who do not have the background to understand the error in thinking about "theory" and "hypothesis;" and (2) they completely discredit themselves to the traditional scientific community, and thus further the schism that already separates fundamental Christian believers from things scientific.

From my point of view this is especially ironic, because there is absolutely no reason why a person cannot believe in the underlying precepts of Christianity and simultaneously accept the modern theory of evolution in its full-blown glory. The God in whom fundamental Christians so ardently believe could be the architect of biological evolution without impacting in any way the fundamentalist Christian concept of original sin and ultimate redemption.

Beam Me Up, Scotty!

In all the episodes of the original "Star Trek" series, not once did Captain Kirk actually use the words: "Beam me up, Scotty!" It might be interesting to examine not only why he never said this, but also why he never could have said it.

Although it is not completely obvious, when we examine something, we really are interpreting the pattern of reflected photons from the object as they fall on the retina of each eye. The process is incredibly complicated—so much so, in fact, that computer scientists have not yet learned how to program even a supercomputer to simulate this with any accuracy or fidelity.

Take a wall, for example. Photons from the sun, which is our light source, reflect—"bounce"—off the wall and fall on our retinas, so that we perceive an image of the wall. If we mentally substitute tennis balls for photons, we can build a mental picture of what is happening. A tennis serving gun that shoots balls at the wall will be our "light" source. By appropriately aiming the gun and observing which balls bounce back and which don't, and also by observing the pattern of the returning balls, we can quite accurately measure the size, distance, and even other gross characteristics of the wall.

Picture a raised pattern on the wall face consisting of components smaller than the tennis balls. By observing the ball dispersal pattern, we can deduce that there is some kind of raised pattern on the wall, but will be unable to determine any of its details.

This analogy is not perfect, because photons act in strange ways, depending on how they are being used and interpreted. Sometimes they act as waves instead of particles, and this confuses things, but for this discussion we will keep just to the particle character of photons.

If we substitute something smaller for the tennis balls—marble-sized balls, for example—then we can reexamine the wall, deducing its finer details. It may also become necessary to fire the balls with more energy in order to get them to bounce back with appropriate information. As the smaller balls hit the raised pattern elements on the wall, how they bounce back will give us much more detailed information about this pattern than we could surmise from the larger tennis balls. Continuing the analogy, as the detail we wish to examine gets smaller, we use ever smaller, more energetic balls to conduct the examination. Eventually, the balls we fire at the wall begin to damage the very structure we are attempting to examine, as the BBs chip away at the plaster designs.

The point here is that no matter what we wish to examine, and no matter what we choose as our examining particle, sooner or later one of two things will always happen. Either the particle is too large to do the job anymore, or the particle is too energetic, so that it disturbs, or even worse, destroys whatever is being examined.

Much that we wish to examine is on the atomic or even subatomic scale. Photons quickly become useless. Electrons work for a while, but they soon also become useless. In fact, sooner or later, all known particles become useless as observing devices. Eventually, when you use an appropriate particle to determine the specific location of another particle, you so completely disrupt the motion of that particle that you have absolutely no idea when it was there (its "momentum"). Conversely, if you use an appropriate particle to determine the exact momentum of another particle, then you lose all information about its location.

Werner Heisenberg was the first scientist to quantify this information into what is now commonly known as the *Heisenberg Uncertainty Principle.* In effect, the exact simultaneous position and momentum of any specific atomic or subatomic particle is forever unavailable. It's just part of how our universe is.

Now back to Kirk and Scotty.

For the transporter to work, it must measure the exact position and momentum of every single atom in the object to be transported, so it can transmit that information to the receiving site for reconstruction. It must make a precise template, and—as we have seen—that is forever impossible.

And that's the real reason why Kirk never said it, because Scotty can't do it!

Free Will and the Cosmic Speed Limit

On September 23, 1971, B. F. Skinner's new book rocked the intellectual world. *Beyond Freedom and Dignity* was a smashing success that seemed to explain some of the hidden mysteries underlying human behavior. Indeed, the author purported to set aside the very concepts of "freedom" and "dignity" as we normally think of them. You change human behavior, Skinner asserted, not by appealing to the "inner person," not by teaching "self-reliance," not by elevating human "freedom" and "dignity," but by changing the human environment, by structuring it so that the only viable outcome is the desired outcome.

Beyond Freedom and Dignity quickly became the justification for, or the reason behind, an entire slew of measures in both the public and private sectors aimed at redirecting human behavior by manipulating appropriate segments of the environment. Conversely, *Beyond Freedom and Dignity* was also vehemently criticized due to its underlying premise, which is that, in the final analysis, free will does not exist. Put another way, whether free will exists or not is irrelevant; what matters is the outcome.

When confronted with the idea that free will does not exist, most thoughtful persons respond by demonstrating some trivial act of free will. Skinner would argue, however, that the sequence of events that led to the free-will act in some way determined that act. In a sense, he postulated an underlying set of micro factors that inevitably determines each macro occurrence. In Skinner's view, these micro factors ultimately are completely deterministic, so that it logically follows that macro events must be determined and, therefore, occur without free will.

Skinner went on to argue that, since one can never completely know these micro factors, one can function as if they did not exist; in other words one may accept free will as a determining variable. He then argued, however, that one can more effectively modify human behavior by understanding and controlling—to whatever degree possible—the underlying micro factors than by appealing to the factors that seem to influence free-will decisions.

In Skinner's view, the viability of free will is not particularly important. Free will is relegated to the uninteresting bag containing things in which we once believed. Free will becomes irrelevant.

It is instructive, however, to reexamine free will as a consequence of the interrelationships between Einstein's General Relativity field equations and the quantum mechanical laws that govern gravity. While it is impossible to explain here the intricacies of these complicated realms of theoretical physics, it is entirely possible to glean some interesting insight from several of the exotic predictions that follow inevitably when these laws are applied in special ways.

One of the consequences of Einstein's law of General Relativity is the probable existence of "wormholes" in the fabric of space-time. Most people know that in some mysterious fashion, nothing can exceed the speed of light. Wormholes, if they exist, may offer a way around this limitation.

First, however, let's examine this cosmic speed limit. It is real. What people usually do not know is the relatively simple reason.

Einstein actually developed two theories of relativity: the Special Theory of Relativity in 1905 and the General Theory of Relativity in 1915. (Now, remember: as used here, "theory" does not mean hypothetical. It means a model-derived solution.) According to the Special theory, matter, the stuff that makes up everything around us—air, furniture, ground, water, cars, etc.—behaves quite differently when it moves at high speed than when it is at rest.

When you fire a bullet from a gun, although it is not at all obvious, the speeding bullet gets heavier. The amount is so small that it cannot be measured by any laboratory device we have, but this is only because a speeding bullet really is moving quite slowly, when compared to the speed of light. If you were to accelerate the bullet so that it was moving at some significant fraction of light speed, its increase in mass would be very apparent. Furthermore, if you were to accelerate it to the speed of light, its mass would become infinite, an obvious impossibility, since it would take an infinite amount of energy to get this infinite mass to light speed.

This characteristic, strange as it seems, is one of the fundamental facts of the universe—things that move fast increase their mass; they get heavier. This becomes a practical matter in a cyclotron, where subatomic particles are accelerated to very high speeds. As their speed becomes a significant fraction of light speed, they become very much heavier, so that the accelerating magnets have to be given a great deal more power just to keep things going.

A second interesting effect for an object moving at very high speed is that it gets thinner in the direction it is moving. As before, this effect can only be observed when the object is moving at a significant fraction of light speed. If you were to move an object at the speed of light, it would become infinitely thin, another impossibility.

This effect also has practical implications in high-speed particle research. A very fast moving particle of known size actually appears thinner than when it is at rest. Sensors must be calibrated to take this into account, or they can't even see the particles.

Another strange effect at high speed is that time slows down for a rapidly moving object. Several years ago, the amount of this slowing was physically measured when a satellite was orbited containing a highly accurate atomic clock, while the twin of the clock remained on the Earth's surface. Even though the satellite's speed was still slow compared to light speed, it was sufficiently fast for the slowing of the satellite's time to be measured by the two identical clocks as their initially synchronized times began to move apart.

Another way to look at this phenomenon is to view an object moving through space-time as a simple vector. Imagine a grid with velocity laid off on the vertical axis and flow of time laid off on the horizontal axis. A real object can be represented as an arrow starting at the zero point, and pointing up into the grid. According to Einstein's Special Theory of Relativity, the length of this arrow or vector is constant, represented by the speed of light. This means that in the space-time continuum (as opposed to just space), all objects have constant motion; all objects move through space-time at exactly the same rate. On the vector diagram, this is equivalent to saying that the object is represented by a vector, an arrow with constant length.

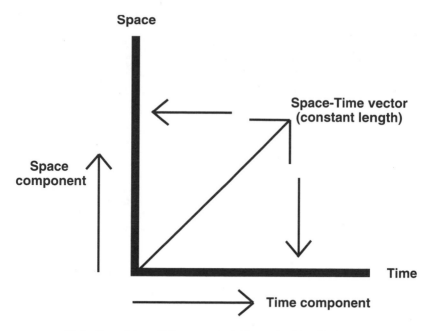

Relationship of Space and Time in the Universe

In our diagram, the direction the vector points and its constant length (which is fixed by the speed of light) determine the amount of the vertical component, the "space" velocity, and the amount of the horizontal component, the "time" velocity. From the tip of the arrow, draw a line straight across to the velocity axis to get the space velocity component. Drop a line straight down from the arrow point to the time axis to get the time velocity component. In effect, the object's total constant velocity through space-time is the "vector sum" of the velocity through space and of the movement through time.

For objects in our normal existence, the vector or arrow on the grid points nearly horizontally, because the object's speed—its velocity component on the vertical axis of the diagram—is very small, even for high-speed aircraft and satellites. Because of this, the

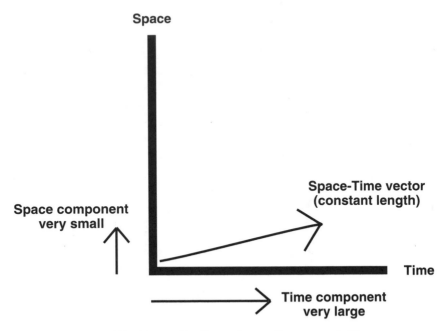

How We Normally Experience Space and Time

vector consists mostly of the time component. Any small changes we make to the vertical axis of the diagram have very little effect on the horizontal part of the vector.

Since the length of the vector does not change, as we add more velocity to the "space" component, to the vertical axis, the vector begins to swing upwards, so that we see increasing reduction of the horizontal component, the "time" element. In other words, as the velocity through space increases, in order to maintain the constant length of the vector, the motion through time decreases.

If we rotate the vector all the way to the vertical, all of its velocity through space-time consists of the vertical component—velocity through space—and the

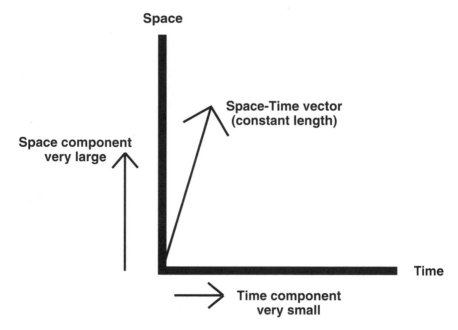

Space and Time at Very High Velocity

object would be moving at the speed of light. None of the vector velocity would consist of the horizontal component—movement through time.

In other words, if an object were to move at the speed of light, time would cease to exist for it, another obvious impossibility.

We see this effect clearly in subatomic particle research, where once again it has practical significance. If you fire a radioactive particle with a half-life of a microsecond at a target, you can move the target far enough away from the source that the particle will decay before it hits the target. But if you fire the particle with a speed that is a significant fraction of light speed, because time slows down for the fast-moving particle, it arrives at the target before it decays, whereas

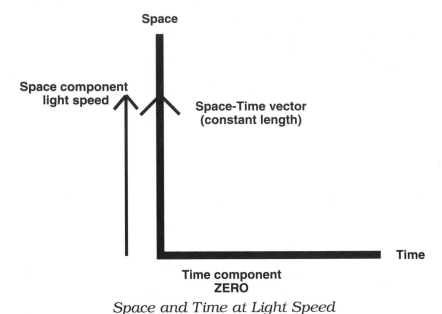

Space and Time at Light Speed

calculations that ignore this effect indicate that it should have decayed before arriving at the target. In other words, the "time-dilation" effect must be considered when running experiments using radioactive high-speed particles.

The Twin Paradox

Here is another, more practical example of how time-dilation can affect real people in the real day-to-day world. Imagine that we live sufficiently far into the future that travel between stars is routinely possible. People can purchase tickets for transport from Earth to the Sirius double-star system, for example, about nine light years distant.

Let us imagine that you are one-half of a twin set—say two brothers. You are both the same age, of course. One of you decides to take the grand tour out to Sirius, stay there for a year, and then come back. The other prudently decides to remain safely on Earth.

In any real example like this, we would have to discuss how we intend to accelerate the starship to near light speed, from where we might obtain fuel, etc. For our thought experiment, however, we'll just assume that somehow humans have developed the necessary technology to accomplish this. We will assume some time during the acceleration and deceleration, during which the traveling twin ages at approximately the same rate as his brother. Of course, during his time in the Sirius system he will also age at the same rate. But for the time spent near light speed both on the outbound and the return trips, the traveling twin's timeline will nearly stop.

If we generously allow six months to accelerate and six months to decelerate on both the outbound and return legs, plus the year in the system, for three years the traveling twin will age at about the same rate as his brother back on Earth. If he really gets close to light speed, the "subjective" time experienced by the traveling twin will be several weeks at most on each leg, say a month and a half out and the same back, for a total of three months, during which time the brother on Earth will age eight years for the outbound leg and another eight years for the return leg. Thus, upon the traveling twin's arrival back on Earth, he will have aged three years and three months, while his twin brother will have aged nineteen years and three months.

The implications of this very real phenomenon are astounding. Once you have accelerated to near light speed, the difference between "rest" time and "subjective" time reaches astonishing heights, so that—at least hypothetically—a traveler could cross a significant part of the known universe and return, having aged only several years, while millions or even billions of years would have passed back on Earth. To people on Earth, or on any other planet for that matter, it would seem a form of time travel, but only moving forward.

The traveler, on the other hand, would experience a normal "subjective" lifetime, but with each trip out and back, would leap into the future by an amount dependent upon how far and how fast the traveler went. This ultimately would develop into two entirely different societies. The one would consist of people living at "rest," with respect to their universe, as we do today. The other would consist of people who continuously leaped forward in time. By properly calculating the jumps and intervals, they would be able to synchronize aging or catch up with another person, or fall behind, but all the while living a normal span of "subjective" life. Yet these people would appear as immortals to people trapped in the "rest-time" universe, since they would appear from time to time during a regular lifetime, without any apparent aging or other signs of time passing.

It may turn out that there is no way to bring about such acceleration to near light speed. If this turns out to be true, then our discussion becomes nothing more than a pleasant distraction. If, on the other hand, we eventually discover how to accelerate to near light speed and maintain ship's integrity, and the million and one other things that will become necessary to accomplish this task, then we humans will be able to spread throughout the known universe. Who knows what we may discover; what we may become?

Each of these effects becomes more pronounced as the object's speed approaches light speed. In fact, at light speed, an object's mass becomes infinite, time stops, and it becomes infinitely thin—things that obviously cannot happen in any real universe.

Hence, in the world in which we really live, nothing can exceed the speed of light—the cosmic speed limit.

How Big Is Big?

We have been throwing around the term "light year" without really explaining how large a light year is. A light year is the distance light travels in a year (remember, light speed is constant). The numbers get so big that they lose meaning, so let's set up a mental picture we can understand. In one second, a beam of light would travel around the Earth about seven and a half times. In round figures that is 186,000 miles in a second. That calculates to just under 670 million miles in an hour; which converts to just under 16.1 billion (thousand million) miles in a day; which converts to somewhat over 5.8 trillion (million million) miles in a year, so a light year is equal to about 5.8 million million miles.

That's a big number, and that didn't help much either.

Look at it this way. Light takes about nine minutes to arrive at the Earth from the sun. It takes about nine years to arrive at the Earth from Sirius, so Sirius is about 526 million times further from the Earth than is our own sun. That probably helps a bit.

Let's try one final analogy. Place a basketball representing our sun at the goalposts of a football field. The Earth would be a pea a foot away. Jupiter would be an orange at about the two-yard line, Pluto—the "edge" of our solar system—would be a speck near the thirteen-yard line, and Sirius would appear as two balls 106 miles away, one about 25 percent larger than our sun and a pea about the size of the Earth. These are relationships we can actually understand.

While we're at it, let's place more of our universe

into this picture. The galaxy in which our sun and all its planets reside is about 100,000 light years across. In the picture we have developed with the basketball and the football field, our galaxy is 1 million miles across, or about four times the distance between the Earth and the moon. And the Andromeda Nebula, which is the closest large galaxy to our own and about 2 million light years from our galaxy, would be 20 million miles away from our basketball, or about one-fifth the actual distance to our sun.

The distances get so large so fast that it is nearly impossible to keep a picture in mind of how all this relates together. If we collapse our example so that the entire galaxy, which in our example extended to four times the distance to the moon, shrinks to the size of a Frisbee, then Andromeda will be another Frisbee at about the seven-yard line. We are part of about thirteen galaxies in a sphere 10 million light years across—in our collapsed example, about forty yards across.

Let's transfer our base of operations to the 50-yard line so we can better visualize what we have: In a 20-yard sphere centered at the middle of the 50-yard line, we have some thirteen Frisbees of various sizes, in various orientations. Now imagine a sphere that extends outwards four and a half football fields in all directions from center field, a sphere nearly 900 yards across— approaching a half-mile in diameter. This sphere in our collapsed example represents the Virgo Supercluster containing our Local Group of thirteen galaxies plus 160 or so other clusters of galaxies.

Time to collapse again; this is still too big to contemplate. So we collapse our half-mile-wide supercluster down to basketball size again, which represents a distance of about 200 million light years. Within a sphere extending three yards out we will find about eighty other superclusters similar to our own Virgo

Supercluster. This six-yard sphere represents a billion (thousand million) light years.

Now, if you extend the current sphere so that it takes in the entire football field and the bleachers, this represents on our scale, the size of the known universe, about 28 billion light years across.

These numbers get so large so quickly that it is nearly impossible not to get lost contemplating them. We started out with a basketball representing our sun and discovered that the Sirius star system was over a hundred miles away and our galaxy extended four times the distance to the moon. The nearest large galaxy was one-fifth the distance to the sun. So we collapsed our galaxy to a Frisbee and located us inside a forty-yard sphere; this Local Group was but a part of the Virgo Supercluster inside a half-mile-wide sphere. So we collapsed again to basketball size and found our supercluster part of eighty other superclusters in a six-yard sphere. Finally, we extended our sphere to include the bleachers, to contain the entire known universe.

Aren't you glad you asked about a light year?

Warp Speed and Free Will

One of the consequences of Special Relativity is that "space" and "time" as we normally think of them really do not exist independently but rather coexist as space-time; they are inseparable as we discussed in the vector diagram example. Every object in the universe is immersed in space-time so that "my space" and "your space" are not the same (which is quite obvious), but also "my time" and "your time" are not the same either. This is not obvious on the time scale we normally work in because of the phenomenon we looked at on the vector grid. In our everyday experience, our "space" velocity component of the space-time vector is very small, so that the vectors all look pretty much the same. That is to say, "my space-time" and "your space-time" are the space-time of the universe.

General Relativity predicts more strange phenomena. In order to get from here to there in our universe, we and everything else must follow the path that a light beam would follow. To us this path appears like a straight line. In fact, the space-time fabric of the universe is quite "curved" whenever large objects occupy it—big stars, for example. It is sometimes possible for especially massive objects to "pierce" the fabric of space-time in such a way that two points that are very far apart in our normal universe can be very close together when viewed through the "pierced" area, called a "wormhole." Imagine a folded piece of paper with two spots far apart on the paper's surface but located so that one spot is directly over the other because of the fold. The surface of the paper is like our normal universe—the spots are far apart on the surface, as a light beam would travel. If you stick a short straw through the folded sheet so that it pierces both spots, this straw is analogous to a wormhole. The nature of wormholes is such that they not only "affect distance" in the universe, they also "affect time." In effect, a wormhole can be thought of as a time machine.

Imagine a wormhole located so that both openings are quite near one another in the normal universe. Imagine that this wormhole has just the characteristics so that an object that enters one end will exit the other end exactly one second before it enters the first end. Imagine that you shoot a billiard ball into the first opening in just such a manner that the slightly older version of the ball that exits the other end strikes the earlier version of itself. One can imagine this to happen so that the original ball misses the opening. Of course, if the original ball misses the opening, then the older version of itself could not possibly exit the other end of the wormhole, which, of course, means that the original ball could not have been deflected . . . an obvious paradoxical consequence that should not be possible in any real universe.

Caltech physicist Kip Thorne and several of his colleagues worked out the detailed quantum mathematical consequences of this thought experiment. They discovered that no matter how you choose to set things up, if you hit the first hole with the ball, the exiting older version of the ball will assist the younger version on its way. It turns out to be impossible to set up a condition where the paradox becomes a reality. No matter from where you choose to start the ball, if the exiting older ball strikes the younger ball, it will enter the hole. Take out the time travel and the quantum effects, put it on a billiards table, and the consequences are as exact: spot the ball, cue it at a specific angle, hit it with a specific force, and there is only one path it can follow.

Free will? Certainly I can choose any starting point, any cueing angle, any speed. These are the domain of free will. What happens after that is the domain of physics—there ain't nothin' I can do about it!

In a sense, Skinner was right; the outcome is determined, but free will sets the conditions. The billiard ball moving through a wormhole doesn't care about free will, but I do. The choices I make determine specific outcomes, which I control by making the appropriate choices. This is true in the bizarre world of relativistic quantum time travel, it is true on the parlor billiards table, and it is true in human society. Some choices inevitably result in undesired consequences; others inevitably result in desired consequences.

The difference is free will.

The Absolute Nature of a Relative Universe

In January 1926 a young Russian-born woman left her home in the budding Soviet Empire and arrived in New York on February 19, after celebrating her twenty-first birthday in Berlin. In five years she became an American citizen, and five years after that she published her first novel, *We the Living*, in the language of her adopted home.

By her death in 1982, Ayn Rand had published several more novels, written several movies, and changed the world in which we live as the founder and chief spokesman for the philosophy of Objectivism, the underlying point of view of the Libertarian Party, the Cato Institute—one of the most influential think tanks on the national scene today—and even Alan Greenspan, former Federal Reserve chairman.

In Rand's own words, one of the four conceptual columns supporting Objectivism is that "reality exists as an objective absolute—facts are facts, independent of man's feelings, wishes, hopes or fears." Stated another way, reality, the external world, exists independent of man's consciousness, independent of any observer's knowledge, beliefs, feelings, desires, or fears.

Between 1926 and 1936, during Rand's first decade in the United States when she formulated this perspective, the scientific world underwent a significant upheaval. Following Albert Einstein's publication of his Special Theory of Relativity in 1905 and his General Theory ten years later, physics underwent a complete overhaul. The world of classical physics, with its neat cause-and-effect relationships, came apart at its seams. The work of Rutherford, Einstein, Planck, Dirac, Schroedinger, Bohr, Heisenberg, and others had revealed a subatomic world that did not seem to react as the classical laws of physics predicted. Instead, researchers found that precise predictions appeared impossible, so that they had to use statistical methods to arrive at solutions that their classically trained instincts told them should have been simple cause-and-effect relationships.

In 1926 and 1927, twenty-five-year-old Werner Heisenberg formulated and refined his Uncertainty Principle, which stated in effect that one could not simultaneously determine the position and momentum of a subatomic particle. He and Niels Bohr spent many hours together discussing the implications of this insight. These discussions were so intense that friends reported Bohr brought Heisenberg to tears on at least one occasion.

By late 1927, Bohr published the Copenhagen Interpretation, which proposed a radical interpretation of Heisenberg's Uncertainty Principle. The Uncertainty Principle stated in effect that the observer was an unavoidable part of the observing process and dramatically influenced the observation. Bohr went beyond this to state that without the observer, the event could not happen. Bohr also said that the subatomic universe of atoms—photons, electrons, and so forth—did not really exist and that these things were no more than a convenient way for humans to visualize theoretical mathematical constructs. This idea took root with the younger generation of physicists, who proselytized it in lectures and classrooms around the world.

The Copenhagen Interpretation troubled several luminaries of this period, among them Einstein and Schroedinger. In a letter to Max Born written on December 4, 1926, Einstein wrote: "The theory yields a lot, but it hardly brings us any closer to the secret of the Old One. In any case I am convinced that *He* does not throw dice."

These discussions, scientific exchanges, and letters produced headlines around the world as nonscientists struggled to come to grips with the concept that "cause and effect" was not real, at least at the subatomic level. The subtler remonstrations of Einstein and his fellow dissenters got lost in the mind-stretching concepts being broadcast by the adherents of the Copenhagen Interpretation. The public entirely missed the nuances of the discussions, hearing only that the observer creates the event.

Calmer voices tried to insert explanations that could be understood by a regular person not versed in the workings of quantum mechanics. One example that surfaced from time to time was that of a physician taking a patient's blood pressure. Inevitably, the explanation went, the physician can only measure the blood pressure of a person having his or her blood pressure measured by a physician. In the real world, there is no way to derive the blood pressure of a person simply doing something normal and unremarkable, such as sitting in a chair reading a book. The measured pressure inevitably includes the effect on the patient's blood pressure of the person taking the measurement. This is completely unavoidable.

In a similar manner, the explanation went, the instrument taking a measurement of an electron's position causes a deflection of the moving electron so that its path always is a direct result of the observation. Without the observation, that particular path will not exist. Furthermore, whatever path is actually taken by the electron cannot be known except in a theoretical sense, since any attempt to determine that path will inevitably result in another path.

Einstein said that God didn't play dice, but he clearly understood that at the current state of knowledge in physics, these questions could only be addressed with statistical functions. He took this as a clear indication that there was another level of knowledge that humans needed to penetrate.

These headline arguments were not lost on young Ayn Rand as she began to think about things beyond herself in her newfound home. She sided with Einstein and Schroedinger, insisting that there really is an external universe, unaffected by the presence of human beings.

During this time, the nonscientific intellectual crowd turned sharply left in its quest for absolute knowledge. In a universe that appeared not to follow any rules, these people concluded that the apparent structures surrounding them manifested themselves as something greater than the sum of their individual parts. Furthermore, since the individual parts followed arbitrary rules, whose very existence was subject to the whim of the observer, the macro universe in which we live must be the consequence of arbitrariness.

Good and evil went out the window of the arbitrary observer, landing on the trash heap of nonessential restrictions. Everything became relative. One idea was as good as another—after all, the observer determined the observation. Right and wrong became two sides of the same coin. Winning through competition mattered less than feeling good by participating. The refrain became: "Anything goes!"

The Second World War temporarily slowed the advance of Relativism, so that the decade of the 1950s was practically "normal," in the sense that people seemed to revert back to prosaic cause-and-effect thinking. The 1960s brought Western culture into conflict with itself. In the United States, the Vietnam War brought this conflict into sharp focus, so that by 1975 the intellectual world was very ready for another way of viewing reality.

Enter Friedjof Capra with his landmark book: *The Tao of Physics: An Exploration of the Parallels Between Modern Physics and Eastern Mysticism.* In this book, Capra started with the Copenhagen Interpretation on one hand and Eastern Mysticism on the other and married them into a unified whole that carried the Relativism theme into every facet of life. The intellectual left found its relativistic view that one idea is equal to another, that everything is relative, completely vindicated.

Since the National Education Association exercises virtual control over what is taught in American schools, and since this organization is, itself, a bastion of the intellectual left, it is hardly surprising that the concept of Relativism has crept into the very fabric of modern America.

Even some very well educated people believe that one scientific point of view is just that, a point of view equal to any other, and steadfastly argue a scientifically untenable idea in the face of incontrovertible evidence.

Relativism has been disastrous for our country. It is high time for the intellectual left to understand that the world of physics really doesn't support the idea that the observer creates the observation. In the universe in which we live, reality really is independent of how we observe it. Our observations affect this knowable reality precisely because it was there before we observed it. Because it is there, we can affect it.

The left has no scientific support for its relativistic belief system. Good and evil are genuine. Right and wrong are real. Competition matters, and winning is better than losing.

The Final Frontier

It happened twice. Space Shuttle *Challenger* exploded seventy-three seconds after liftoff on January 28, 1986, killing all seven astronauts aboard. Space Shuttle *Columbia* broke up on reentry and fell to Earth on February 1, 2003, killing all seven astronauts aboard. These two space shuttle disasters caused a lot of people to stop and reconsider America's space effort. We are expending a great deal of money for the privilege of watching a few individuals spend a limited number of hours in orbit around this planet. What's it all about? Why are we doing this? What is the benefit?

There are plenty of scientists who disapprove of the space program. Prof. Robert Parks from the University of Maryland, for example, wrote in *Ad Astra*, the official journal of the National Space Society, that "if people want to live in harsh environments, let them colonize Antarctica or the bottom of the oceans" instead of a space station. He also "cannot imagine any resources that would justify the costs of space travel to retrieve them." Professor Parks seemed to speak for an influential segment of the scientific community.

On FOX News' "Miller Time," commentator Dennis Miller recently declared that we should set aside the space program for the time being, in favor of more important projects here on Earth. His arguments were amusing (as usual), but thought provoking as well.

If this is the prevalent view, then what are we doing out there?

This question can best be answered by first understanding a typical scientist's perspective. A scientist asks difficult questions about the universe, and then collects data wherein he hopes to find some of the answers. The key word here is data, followed closely by questions. A good scientist would never waste grant money sending a human to collect information that a machine could get for much less. A good scientist cannot be concerned with exotic equipment that may be coming down the pike—he must make the most efficient use of what is at hand. Such equipment frequently is obsolete and second rate.

It is, therefore, easy to understand a researcher's

resentment when he sees $10 million go up in rocket-exhaust fumes to launch a billion-dollar shuttle into near-Earth orbit, when he could have spent a total of $2 million to launch a deep-space probe that would send back valuable information for several years.

The point these good folks have missed is that space travel is not about science—it's about horizons.

Five hundred years ago, people understood this principle clearly. The oceans presented a very difficult barrier, with horizons that seemed to extend indefinitely. Over time, however, humankind discovered that our planet is limited. Today we are genuinely concerned that our presence on this planet may be altering it for the worse. Our planetary horizons have all but vanished. I was one of the lucky ones, spending a year in the uncharted wilderness of Antarctica. For most people today, however, the sense of "beyond the horizon" is something they will never experience personally.

Should this sense of limited horizons become pervasive, our society will stagnate and collapse into itself. Examine our world today. Note the sense of despair and discouragement that seems to permeate the fabric of our culture.

We need infinite horizons. In the words of a popular television program, we need the certainty that some of us will always be able to "go where no one has gone before."

The universe we live in has no limits in the sense that we normally deal with such things. No matter how far we extend ourselves, there always will be another horizon. The survival of our species ultimately depends on this. So long as we can face the unknown, so long as we can challenge the limits of our existence, so long as we can focus on a distant horizon, humans will continue as a functioning element in our incredible cosmos.

Humankind is taking the first faltering footsteps from its cradle—and Parks, Miller, and other Chicken Littles would decry the cost of our shoes.

CHAPTER 13

The Chicken Little
Factor

I started sharing my thoughts in a column in my local newspaper back in the mid-1980s. I titled my weekly column "Thrawn Rickle," from ancient Scottish, where *thrawn* means stubborn and a *rickle* is a loose, dilapidated heap. I saw myself as an opinionated but informed gadfly who took on the distortions and outright lies being foisted on the public.

"Thrawn Rickle" developed a life of its own. It got picked up by several regional newspapers and eventually became a regular feature in one of the nation's oldest periodicals, *The Truth Seeker.*

At the birth of "Thrawn Rickle," there was no Internet, no World Wide Web. The personal computer—the now-ubiquitous PC—had only recently made its debut. Serious PC users still argued the merits of DOS (Disk Operating System) over CP/M (Control Program for Microcomputers), and Bill Gates was still on his way to becoming the world's richest man.

On the other hand, kids who were born when Neil Armstrong first stepped on the moon—including mine—were already in their mid-high-school years. And Jacques Piccard and Donald Walsh had made their historic seven-mile descent to the floor of the Challenger Deep over a quarter-century earlier.

The time span between Galileo's first primitive telescope observations and the launching of the Hubble Space Telescope is 380 years. And yet the time between the Wright Brothers' first flight at Kitty Hawk and Armstrong's historic step is only 66 years.

When I returned from my year at the South Pole, the world's fastest computer was a large, refrigerator-sized, liquid-nitrogen-cooled monster built by Cray—at a cost of millions. Today's G-5 PowerMac leaves that Cray in the dust for less than two thousand dollars, and if you wish to spend just a bit more, you can purchase a PC with a dual-core processor that will blow away the G-5.

When "Thrawn Rickle" first appeared, I could pretty well keep abreast of scientific developments—at least the major ones. Today, I receive hundreds of science- and engineering-related XML feeds into my e-mail inbox each day, along with hundreds of current-events-related feeds. Even a cursory review is becoming impossible.

It is no wonder, therefore, that agenda-driven special interests have assumed the task of filtering this massive amount of information. What the average American sees and hears is not so much what actually happened as what this or that special-interest wants him or her to know.

Is it any wonder that the average American is confused about global warming or the ozone layer or nuclear power? Is it surprising that no one really understands how government impacts the flow of goods and services? Can we really prevent war simply by not fighting—by thinking peace? Is the ethnic makeup of a classroom really more important than how well its members can read, write, and calculate?

Are you really surprised that a modern young person can seriously wonder about contaminating space with plutonium or be concerned about the astrological implications of landing a spacecraft on Saturn's moon Titan?

The Cold War is over. The global greenhouse is not out of control, the ozone layer is still there, and—with a bit of luck—I will live to see men return to the moon and walk the surface of Mars. And maybe, just maybe, I can go there too.

The sky is not falling—never has, never will.

Bibliography

Ad Astra. Washington, D.C.: National Space Society.

Arnold, Ron, and Alan Gottlieb. *Trashing the Economy.* Bellevue, Wash.: Free Enterprise Press, 1993.

Bulletin of the Atomic Scientists. Chicago: Educational Foundation for Nuclear Science.

Capra, Friedjof. *The Tao of Physics: An Exploration of the Parallels Between Modern Physics and Eastern Mysticism.* New York: Random House, 1991.

Christian Science Monitor. Boston: First Church of Christ Scientist.

Cleveland Plain Dealer.

Consumer Alert Comments. Washington, D.C.: Consumer Alert.

Coulson, Andrew J. *Market Education: The Unknown History.* Somerset, N.J.: Transaction Publishers, 1999.

Erlich, Paul R. *The Population Bomb.* Mattituck, N.Y.: Amereon, 1976.

"FOX News." New York: Fox News Network.

From the Wilderness. Sherman Oaks, Calif.: From the Wilderness Publications.

Life. New York: Life, Inc.

Los Angeles Times.

Mensa Bulletin. Arlington, Tex.: American Mensa, Ltd.

The Michigan Review. Ann Arbor.

Microsoft Encarta Online. Redmond, Wash.: Microsoft.

A Nation at Risk. Washington, D.C.: U.S. Government Printing Office, 1983.

A Nation Still at Risk: An Education Manifesto. Washington, D.C.: Thomas B. Fordham Foundation, 1998.

New York Times.

Office of Response and Restoration of the National Oceanic and Atmospheric Administration (NOAA).

O'Toole, Randal. *Reforming the Forest Service.* Washington, D.C.: Island Press, 1987.

The Quill. Indianapolis: Society of Professional Journalists.

Rand, Ayn. *We the Living.* New York: Random House, 1972.

Ray, Dixy Lee. *Environmental Overkill.* Lanham, Md.: National Book Network, 1993.

Ray, Dixy Lee, and Louis R. Guzzo. *Trashing the Planet.* Lanham, Md.: National Book Network, 1990.

Saturday Review. New York.

Seattle Times.

Skinner, B. F. *Beyond Freedom and Dignity.* New York: Random House, 1971.

"Thrawn Rickle." www.argee.net.

Time. New York: Time, Inc.

The Truth Seeker. San Diego.

Washington Post.

Wylie, Phillip. *An Essay on Morals.* 1947. Reprint, New York: Rinehart, 1951.

Index

WITHDRAWN